nicolas

pascal girard

Translated by Helge Dascher

DRAWN AND QUARTERLY

INTRODUCTION
Pascal Girard

I drew *Nicolas* in the spring of 2006 (I think) in less than three days. At the time, I was just starting to draw comics and I wanted to keep a sketchbook as an exercise. I had recently read *AEIOU: Any Easy Intimacy* by Jeffrey Brown and wanted to use his type of narration—life vignettes told in the simplest way, often two panels to tell a moment (big or small). I decided to use my own life (so I didn't have to bother with making a story from scratch). I used the impact of the death of my brother because I had a lot of material that spanned many years of my life. I made a list of moments (big and small) and bought a small sketchbook during my workweek.

During the weekend, I drew the whole book directly in ink, without a script or pencils. It was a pretty relaxed weekend and I still had time to do other things. I guess I was happy with the result and decided to send it to Jimmy Beaulieu—friend, cartoonist, and my first publisher.

Jimmy got back to me with kind words. We were already working on my first book at the time (*Dans un cruchon*, which came out five months before *Nicolas*).

I'm sure a part of me thought that it would be published when I drew it, but frankly, *Nicolas* was first and foremost a personal exercise.

The book was received better than expected and really launched my cartoonist career. And honestly, it happened way too fast: I remember receiving contracts and offers too big for someone who just started making comics.

When I look at the book today, I'm kind of shocked by how raw and unpolished it is. I'm surprised that it even got published. At the same time, I'm pleased by the honesty of it. I don't think I could make a book like this today. When I drew it, I was still unpublished and my readership was limited to family and friends.

For the new edition, I decided not to touch the original but to add a new complementary story. I chose to work in the same way: in a small sketchbook with no script. When I first started to work on those new pages, I didn't know what the story would be. I knew that it would be vignettes from my life related to the same topic, covering things that happened after *Nicolas* was published, but no more than that. I was surprised (somewhat) when I realized that it was all about my other brother, Joël. I followed that route and made a new story.

I reworked and redrew some of the pages. It took approximately two weeks (with a full-time job) to do it—so *way* more than the time spent on *Nicolas*.

I tried to be as honest as I could with ten years of cartooning experience.

nicolas

BEFORE

CLK
CLK
Aw, come on! This isn't working!
CLK

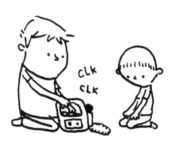

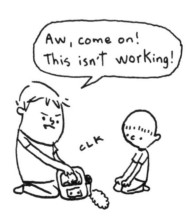

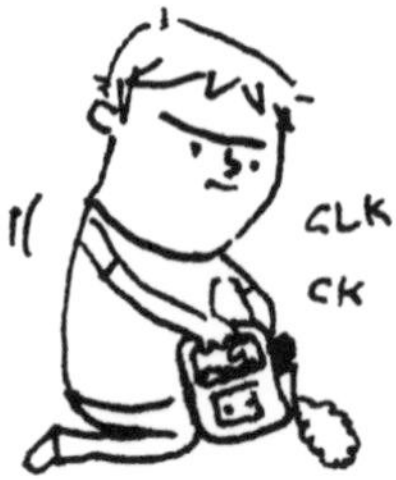
CLK
CK

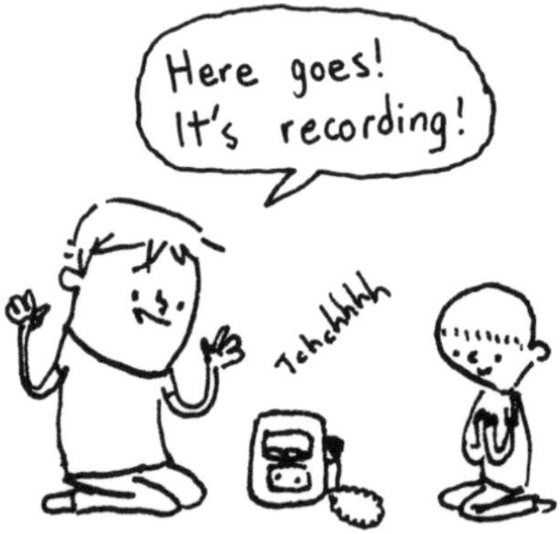
Here goes! It's recording!
Tchchhhh

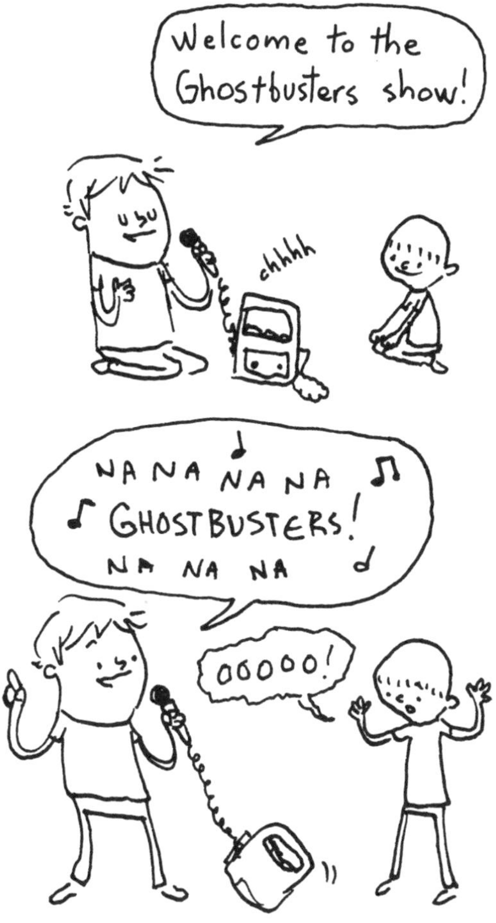
Welcome to the Ghostbusters show!
chhhh
NA NA NA NA
GHOSTBUSTERS!
NA NA NA
OOOOO!

AFTER

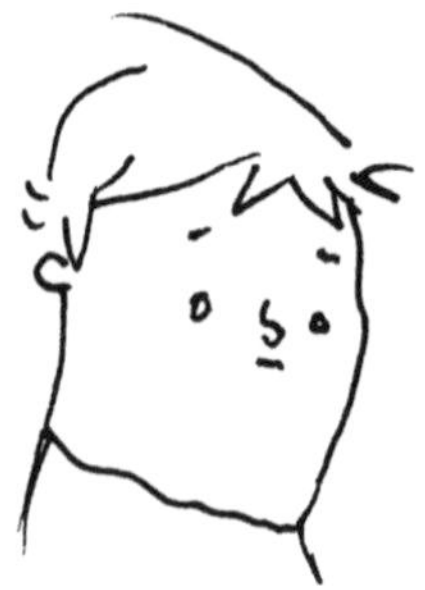

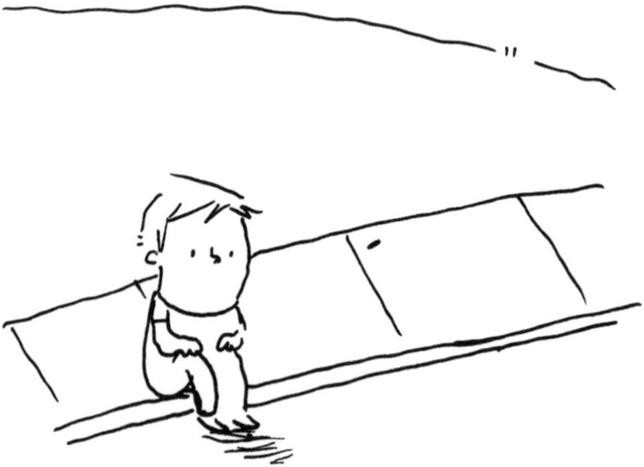

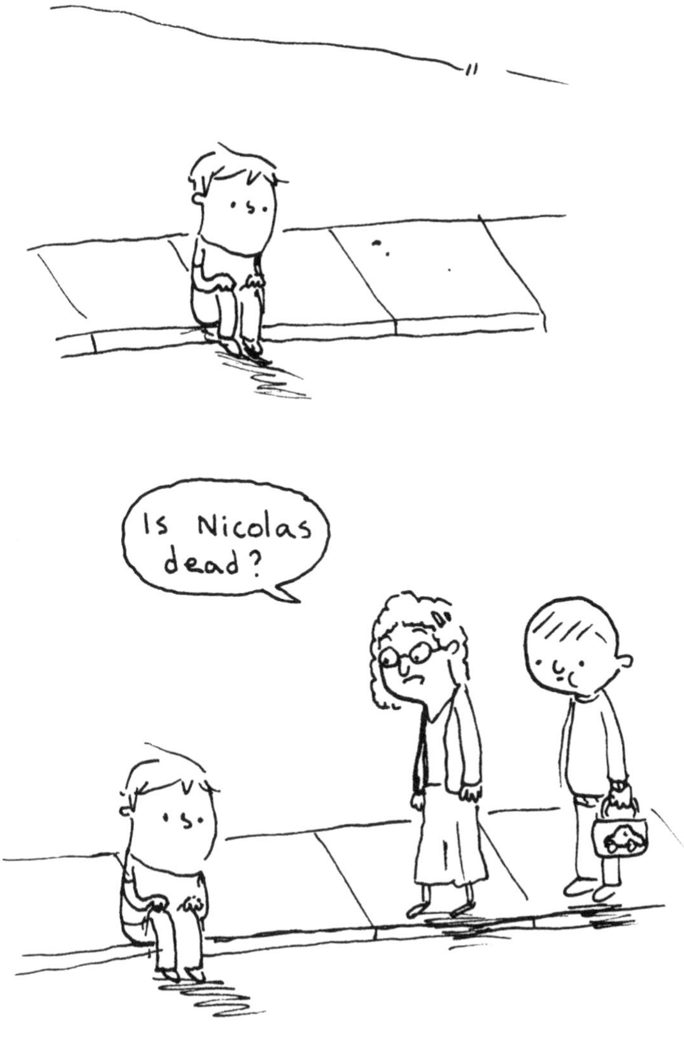
Is Nicolas dead?

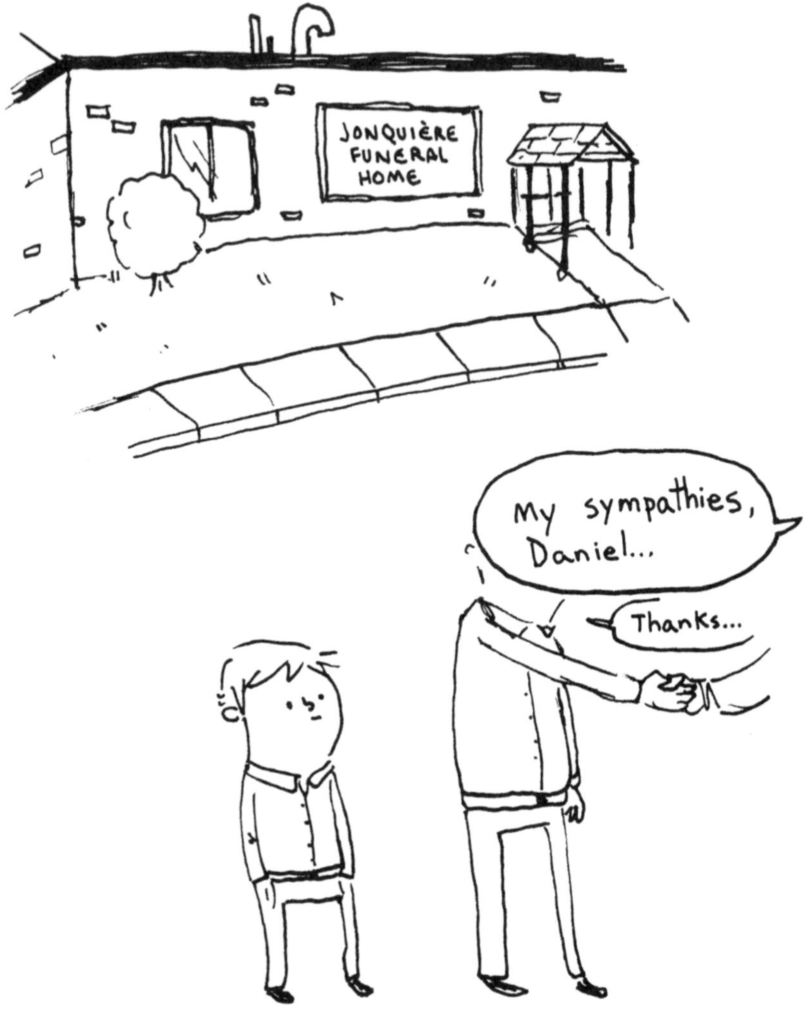
JONQUIÈRE
FUNERAL
HOME
My sympathies, Daniel...
Thanks...

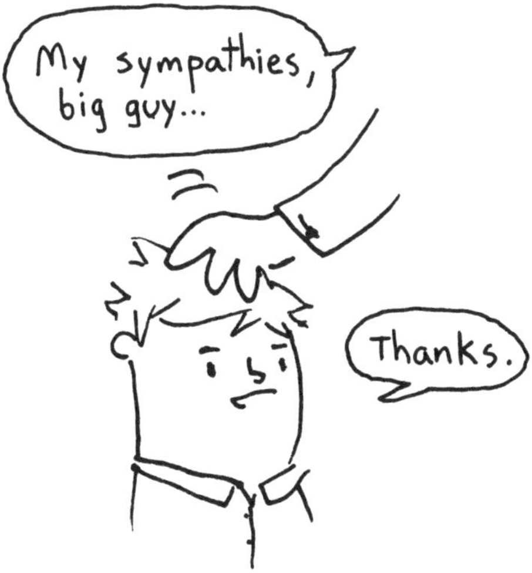
My sympathies, big guy...
Thanks.

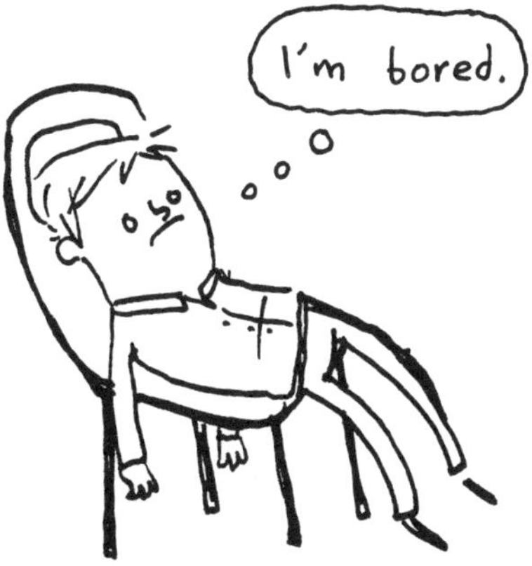
I'm bored.

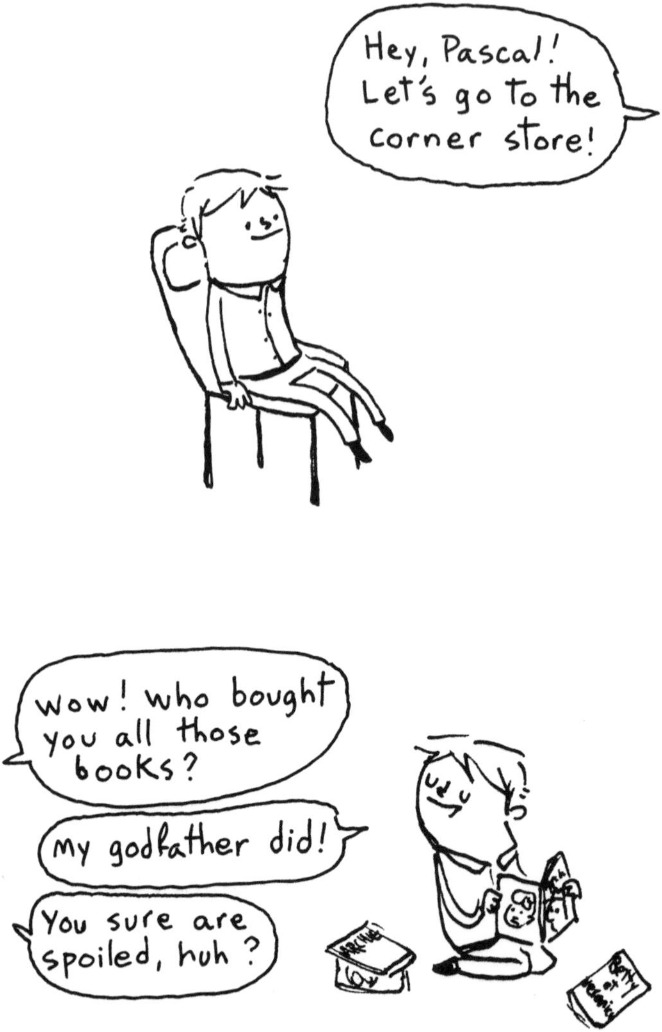
Hey, Pascal! Let's go to the corner store!
wow! who bought you all those books?
My godfather did!
You sure are spoiled, huh?

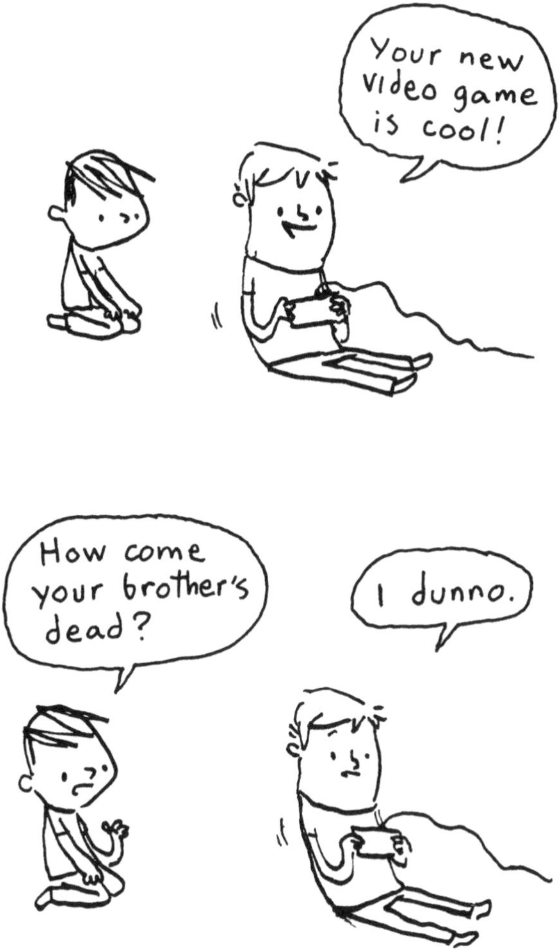
Your new video game is cool!
How come your brother's dead?
I dunno.

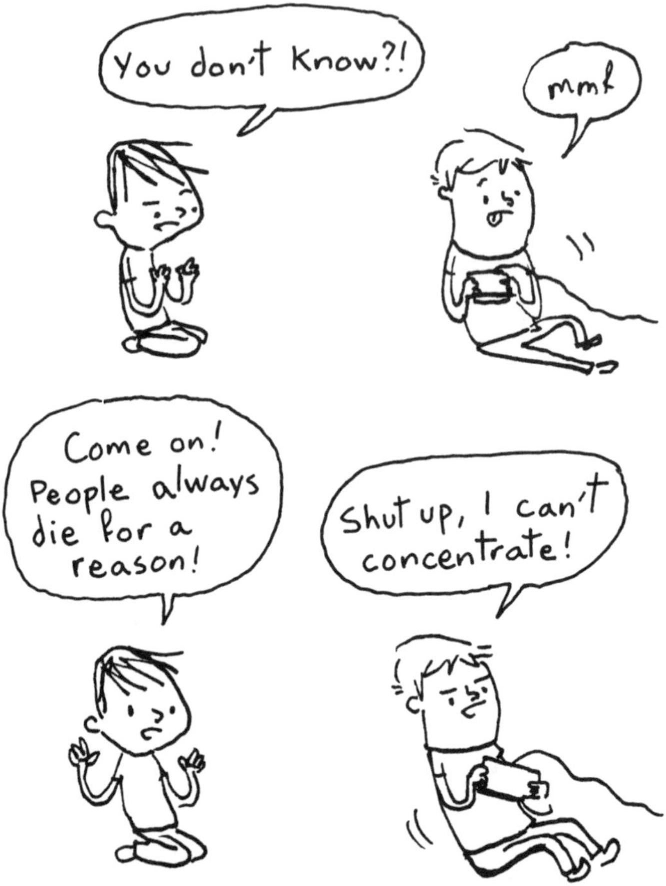
You don't know?!
mmf
Come on! People always die for a reason!
Shut up, I can't concentrate!

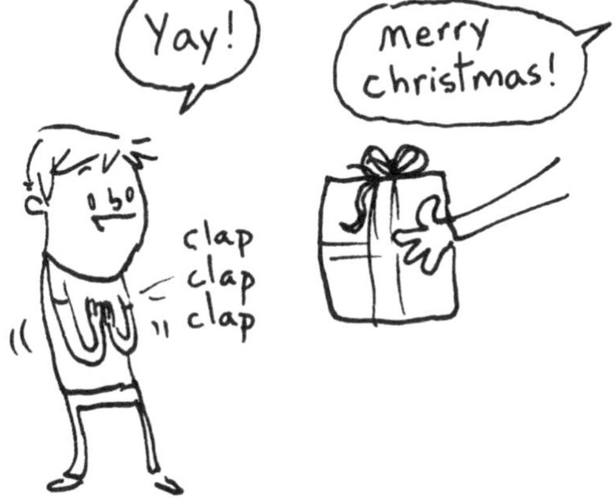
Yay!
merry christmas!
clap
clap
clap
clap

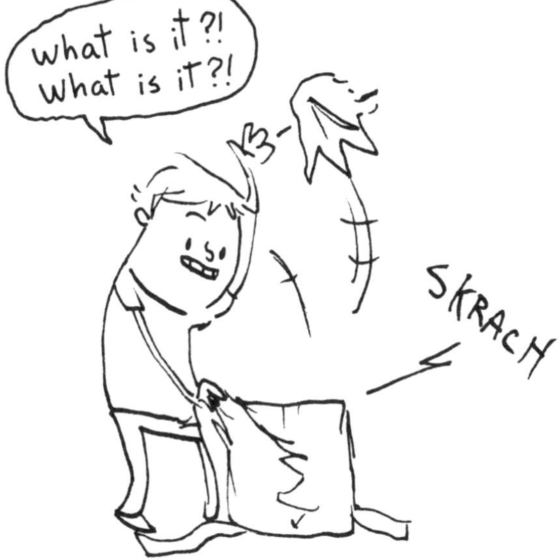
what is it?!
what is it?!
SKRACH

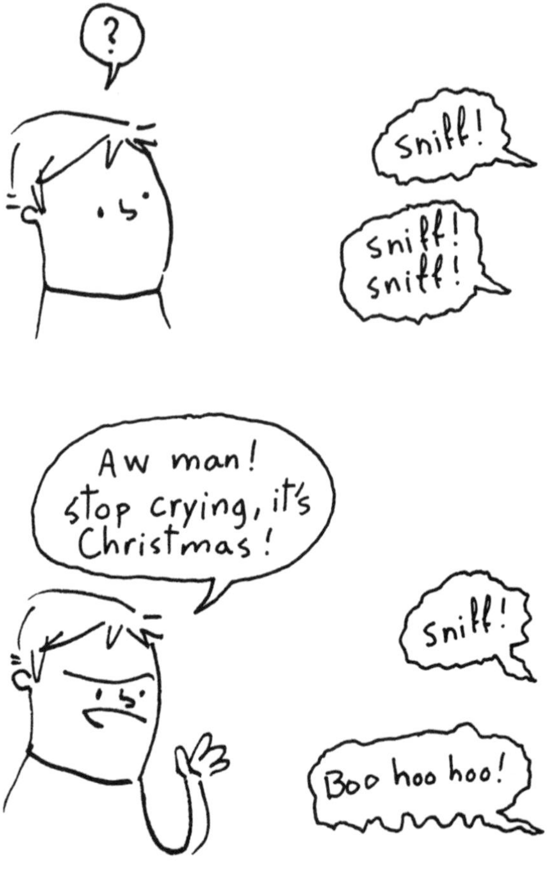
?
Sniff!
Sniff!
sniff!
Aw man!
stop crying, it's
Christmas!
Sniff!
Boo hoo hoo!

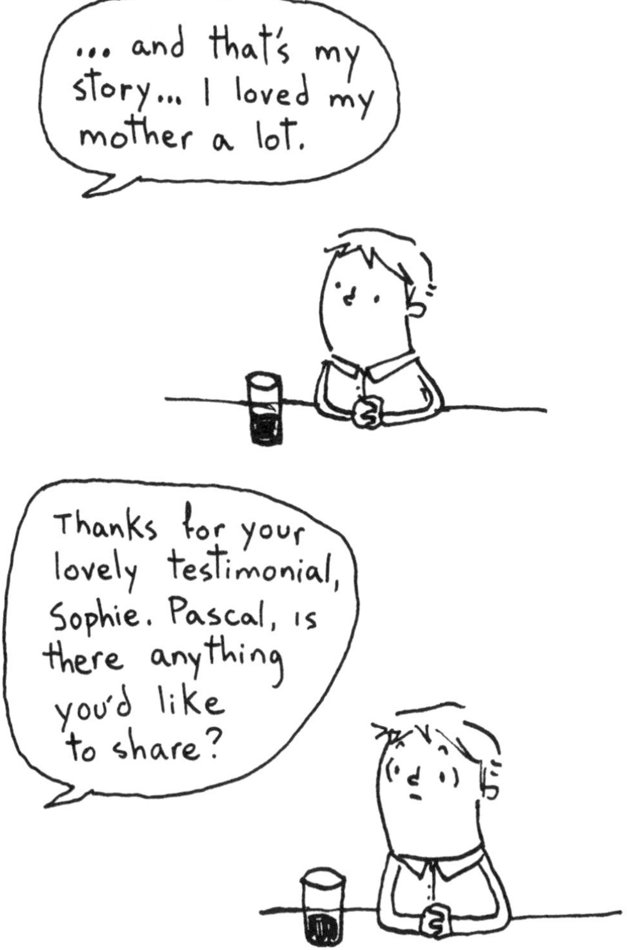
... and that's my story... I loved my mother a lot.
Thanks for your lovely testimonial, Sophie. Pascal, is there anything you'd like to share?

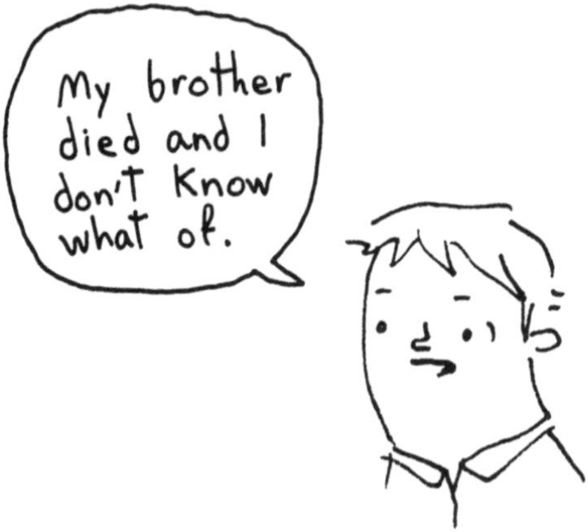
My brother died and I don't know what of.

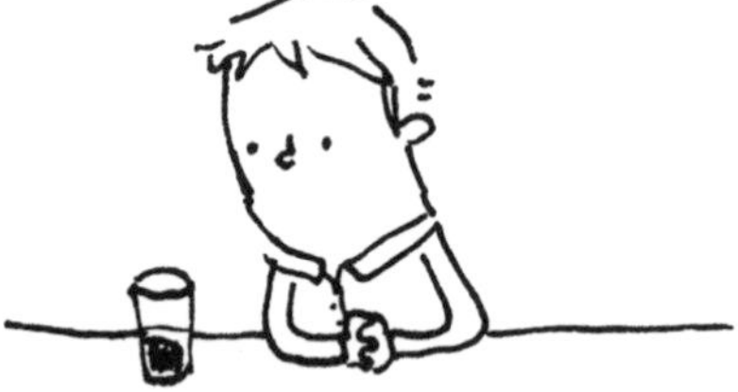

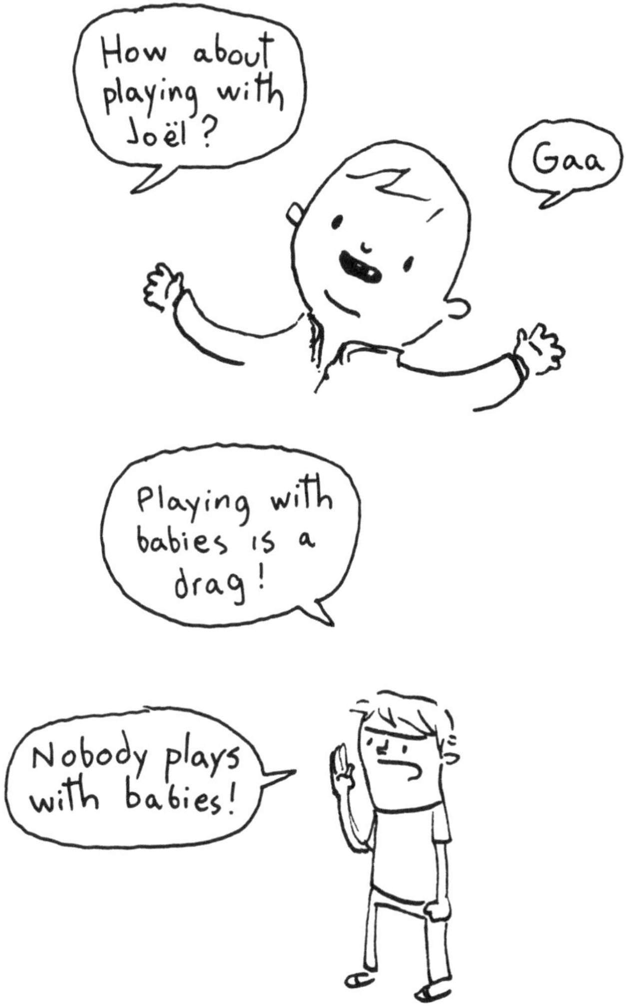
How about playing with Joël?
Gaa
Playing with babies is a drag!
Nobody plays with babies!

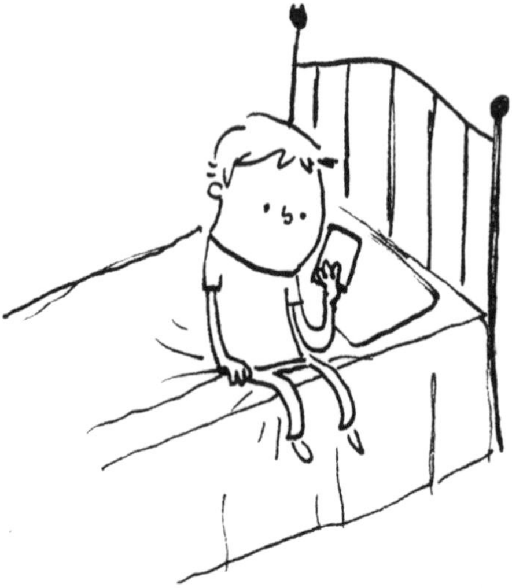

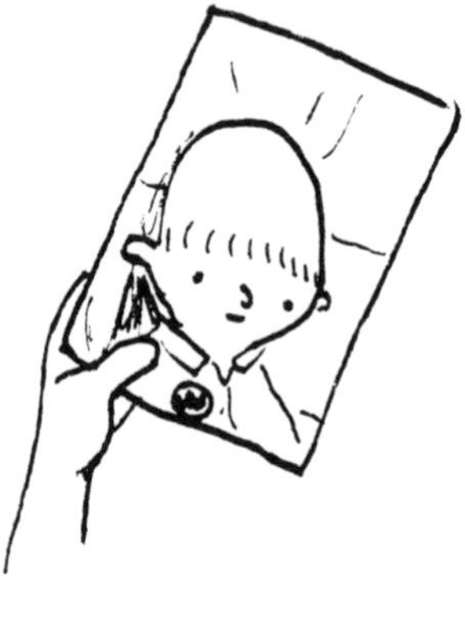

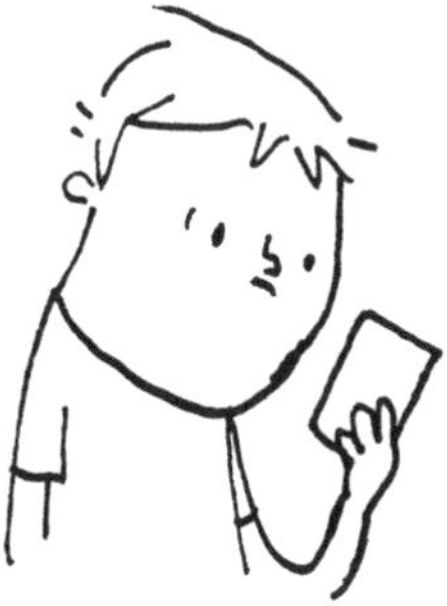

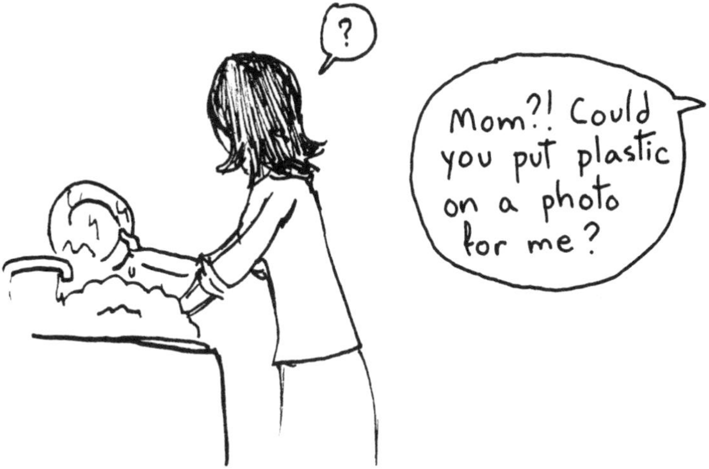
?
Mom?! Could you put plastic on a photo for me?

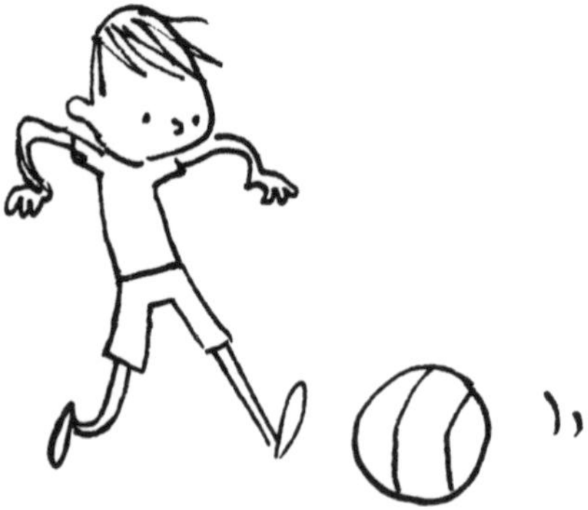

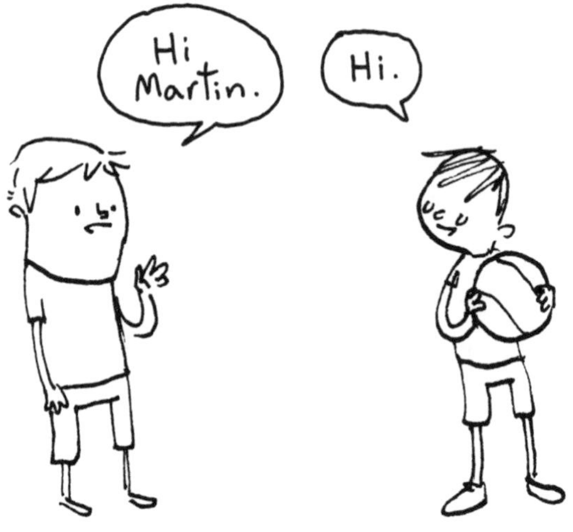
Hi Martin.
Hi.

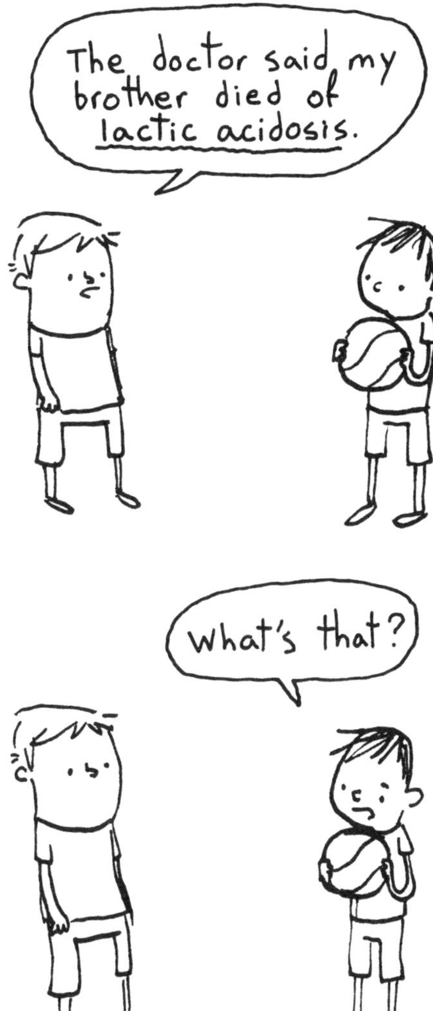
The doctor said my brother died of lactic acidosis.
What's that?

Pascal... I Know you would have liked to see him one last time.
You know what gave him the strength to get through all those shots?

We told him he'd be back home with you soon...
And even though it was hard, he put up with the shots like a big boy.

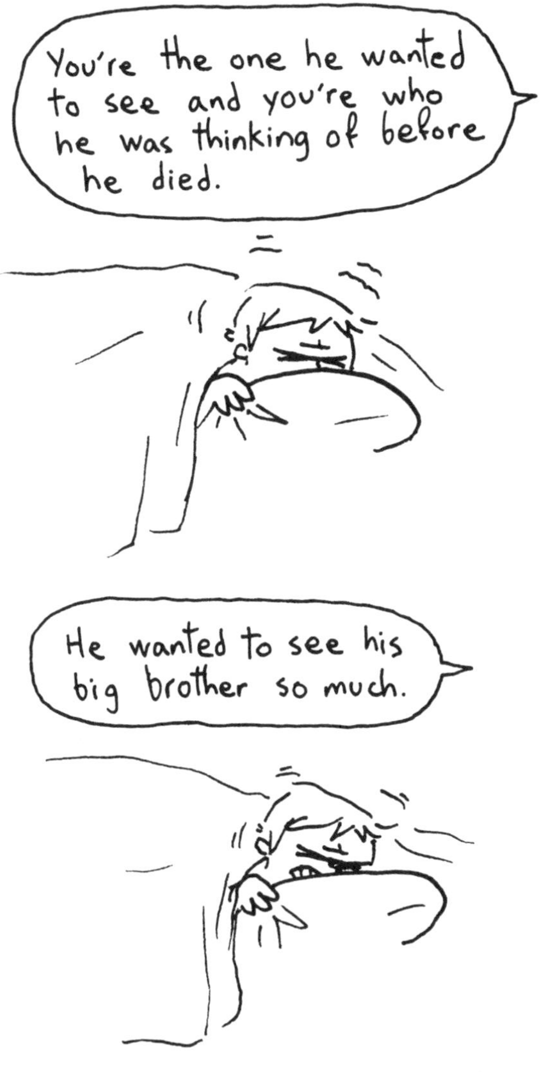
You're the one he wanted to see and you're who he was thinking of before he died.
He wanted to see his big brother so much.

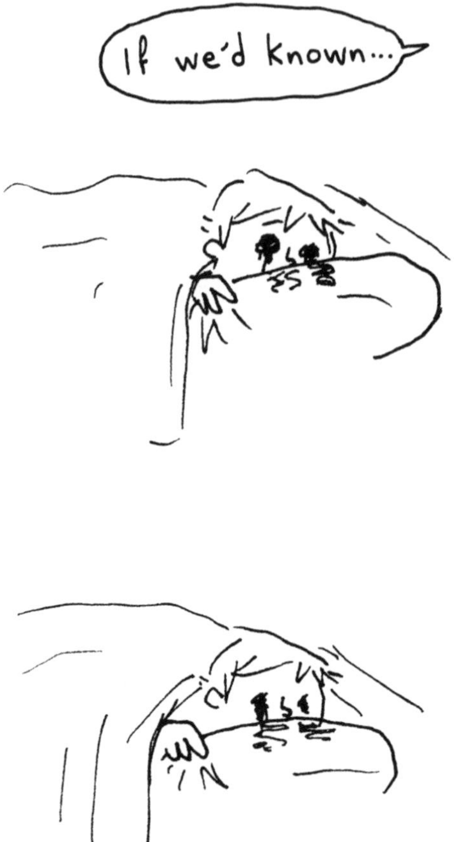
If we'd known...

Tchiik
Tchiik

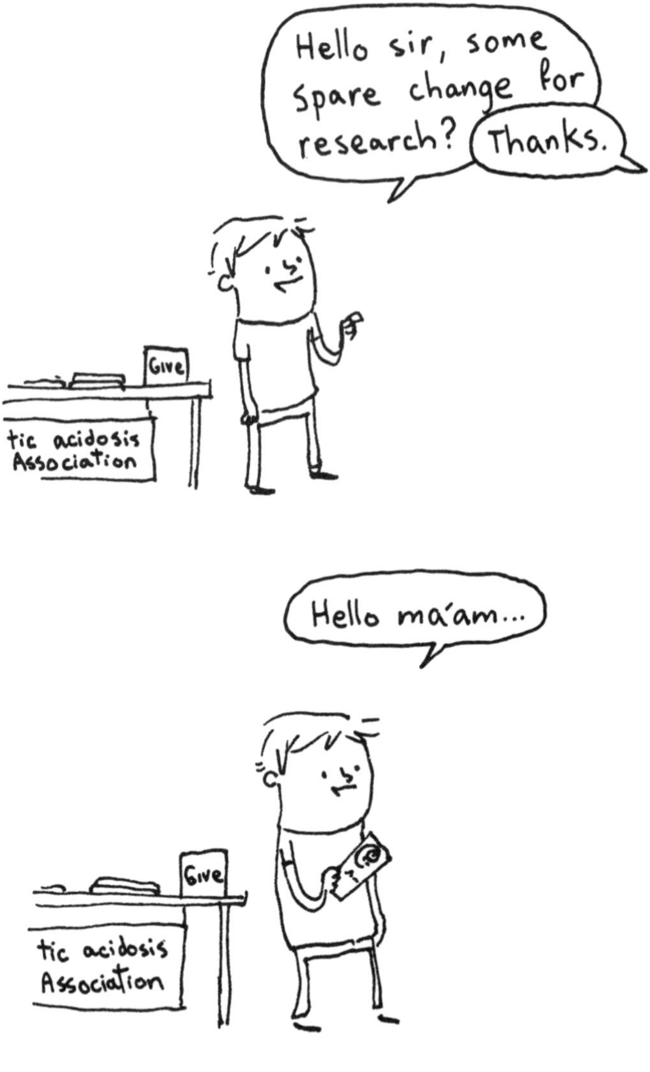
Hello sir, some spare change for research?
Thanks.
Give
tic acidosis Association
Hello ma'am...
Give
tic acidosis Association

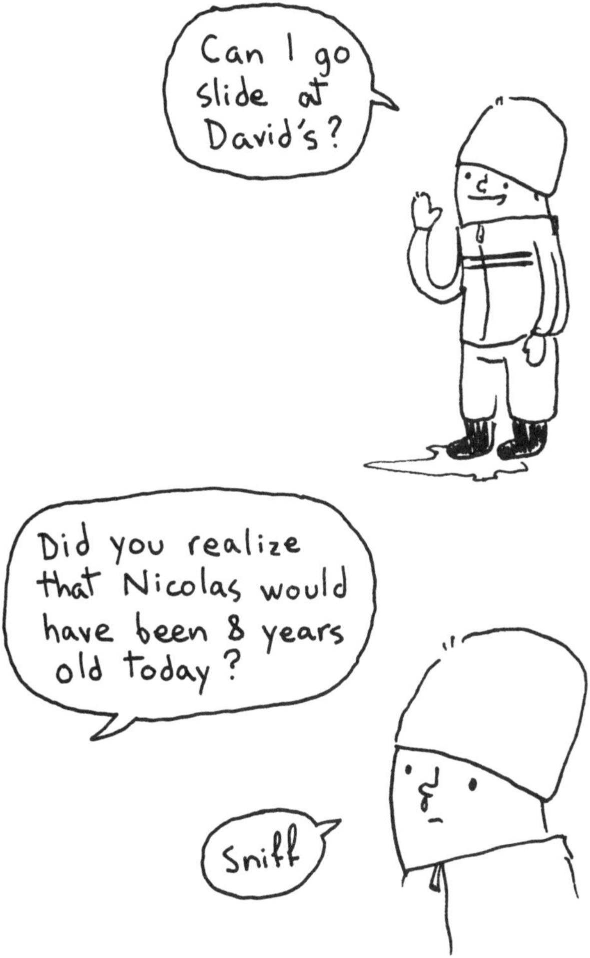
Can I go slide at David's?
Did you realize that Nicolas would have been 8 years old today?
Sniff

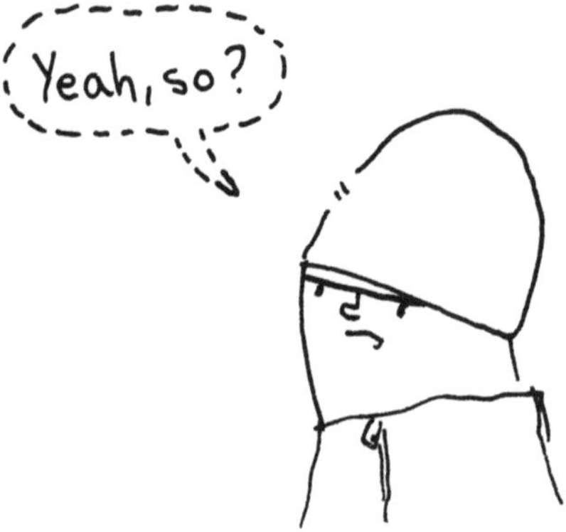
Yeah, so?

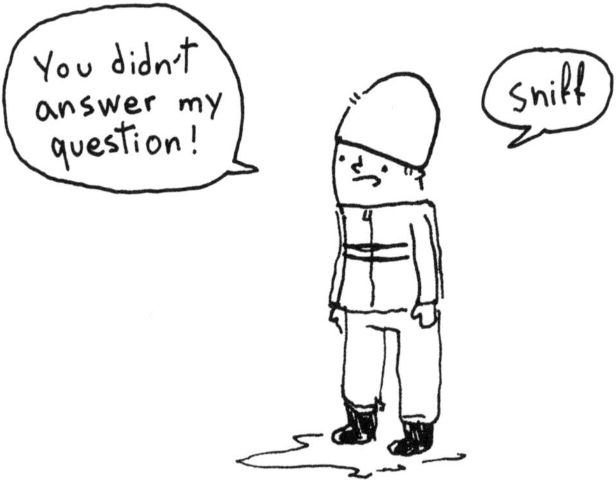
You didn't answer my question!
Sniff

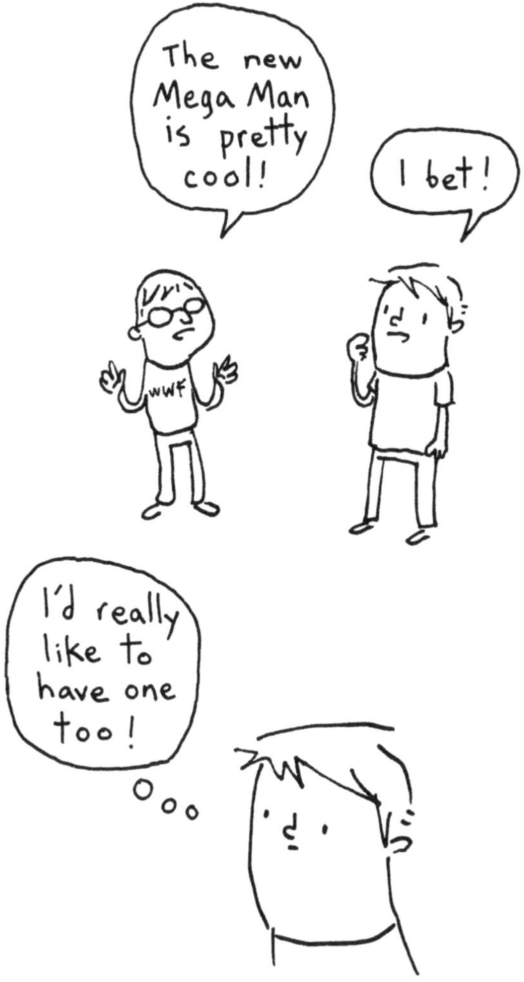
The new Mega Man is pretty cool!
I bet!
WWF
I'd really like to have one too!

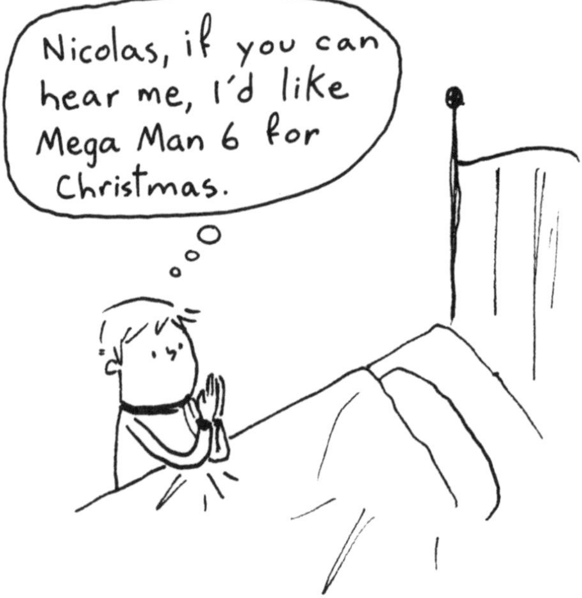
Nicolas, if you can hear me, I'd like Mega Man 6 for Christmas.

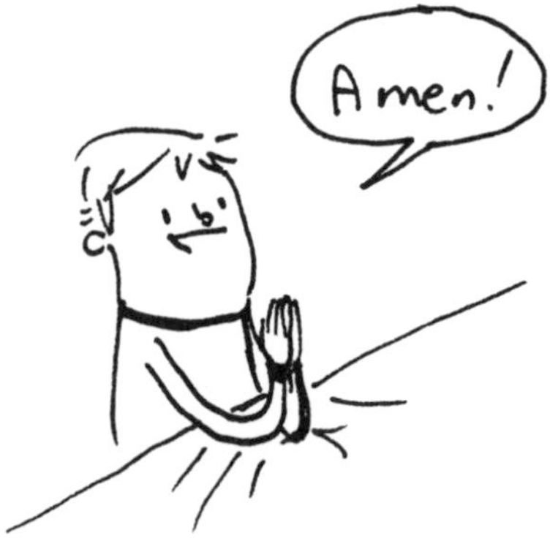
Amen!

Tomorrow,
high
School.

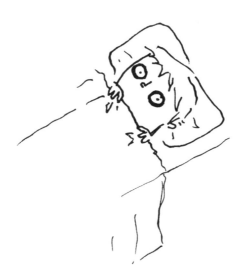

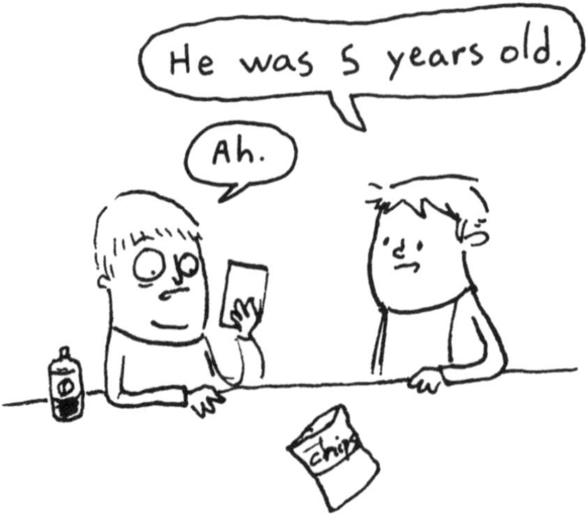
He was 5 years old.
Ah.
chips

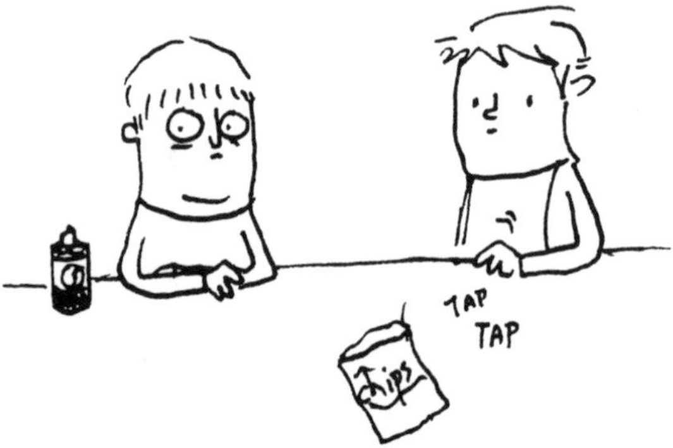
TAP
TAP
chips

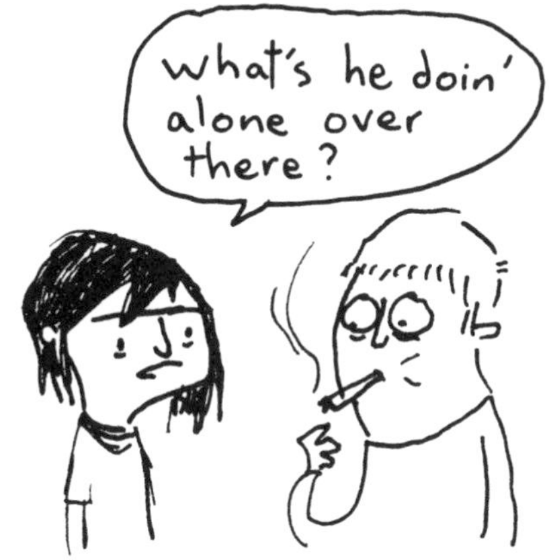
what's he doin' alone over there?

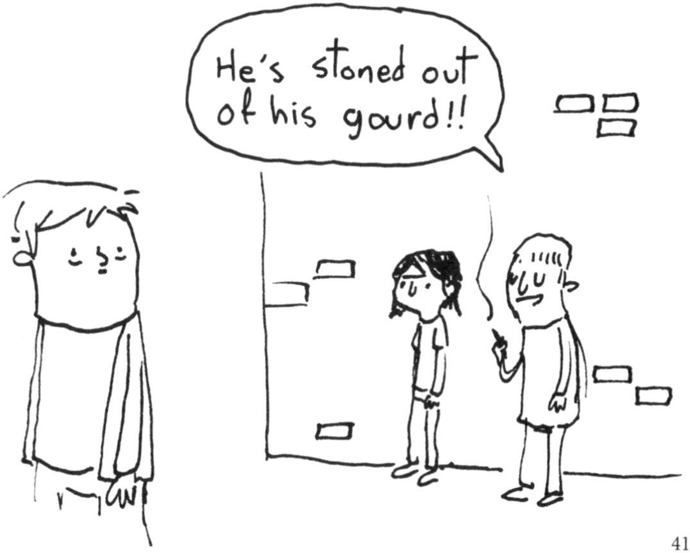
He's stoned out of his gourd!!

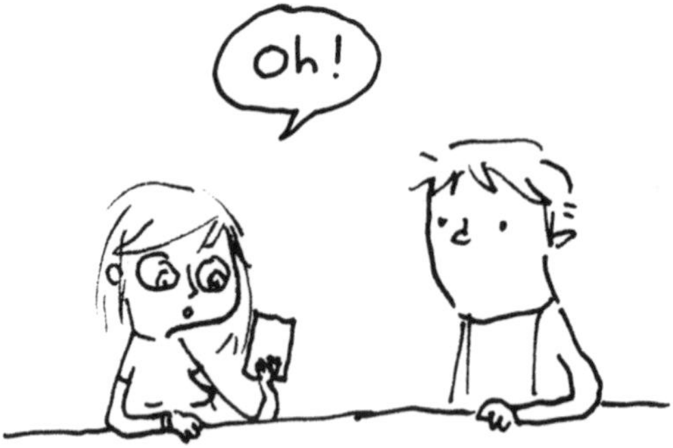
Oh!

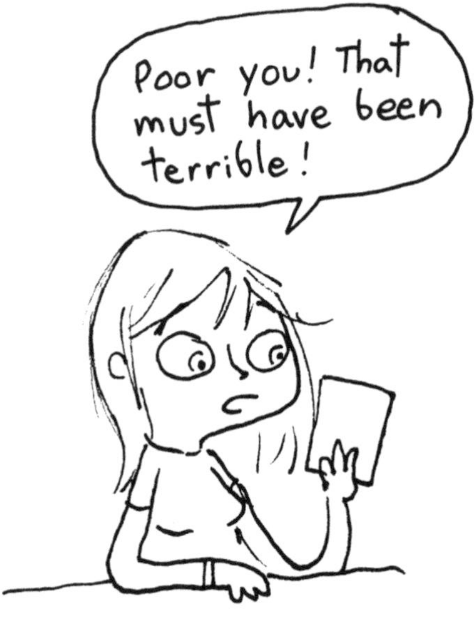
Poor you! That must have been terrible!

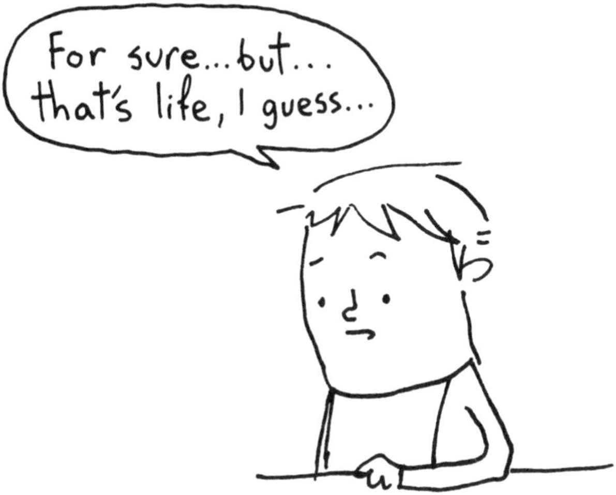
For sure...but...
that's life, I guess...

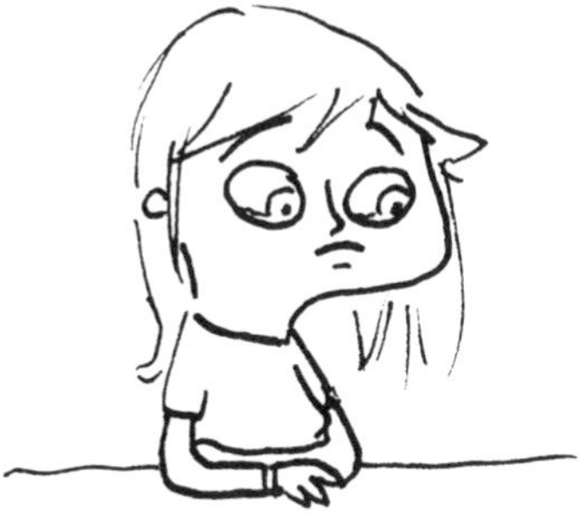

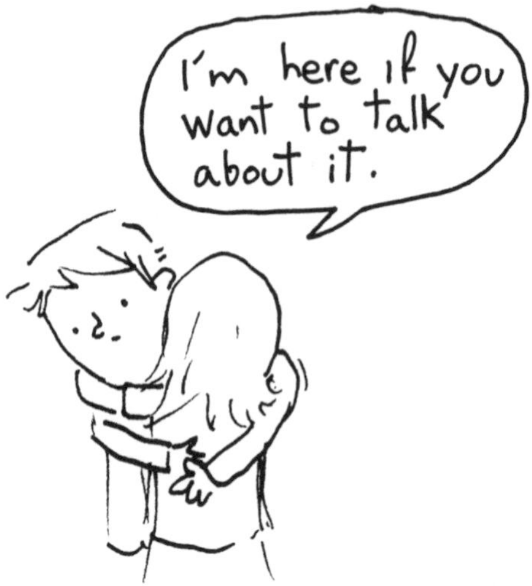
I'm here if you want to talk about it.

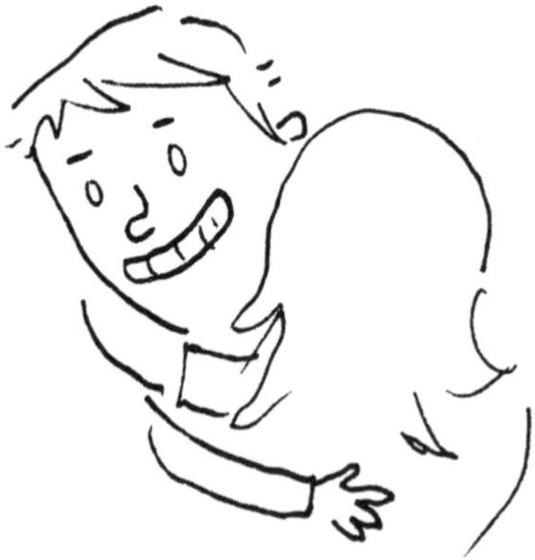

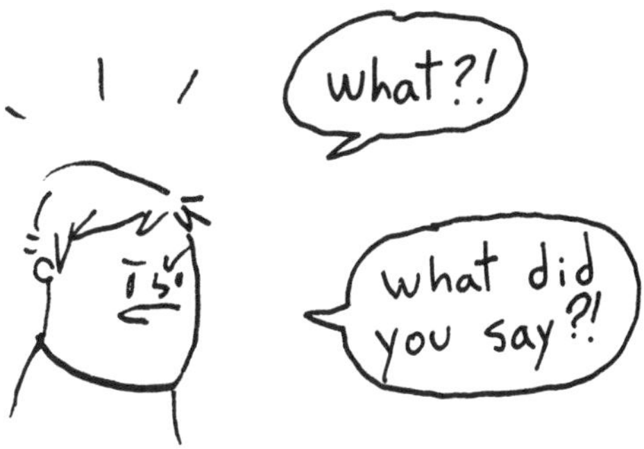
what?!
what did you say?!

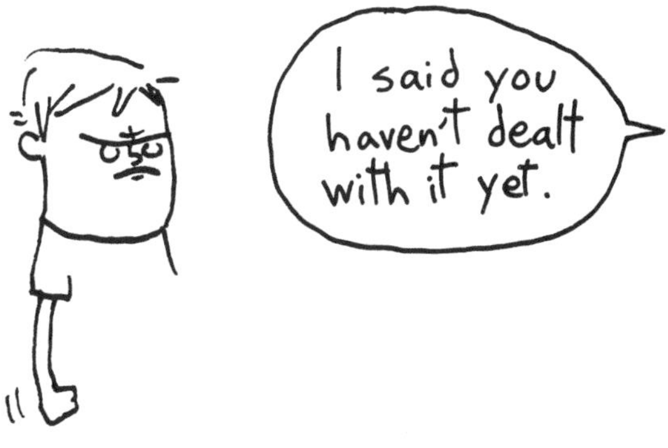
I said you haven't dealt with it yet.

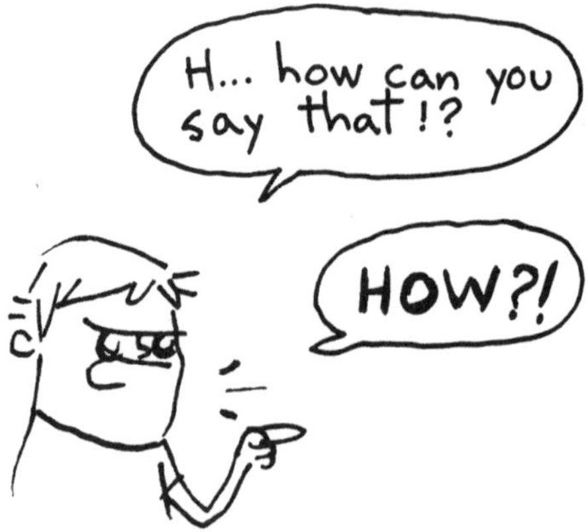
H... how can you say that!?
HOW?!

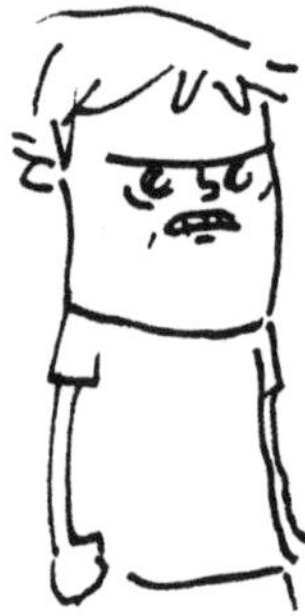

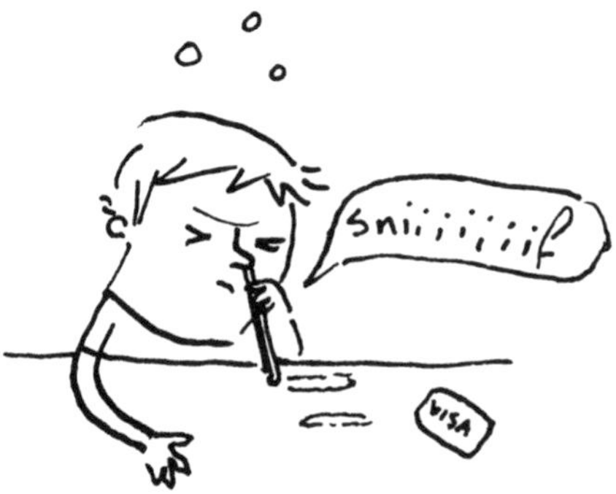
sniiiiiiiif
VISA

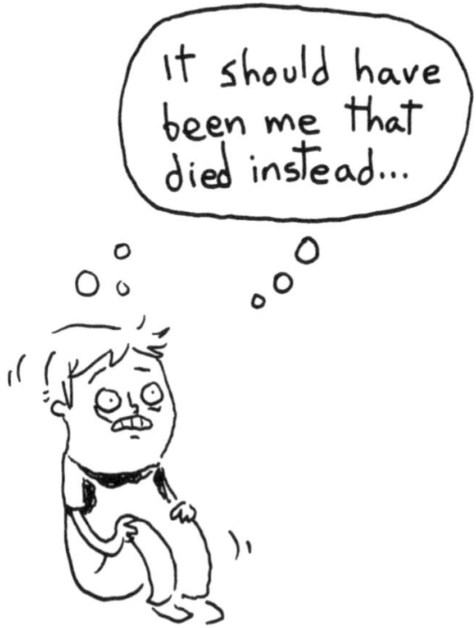
It should have been me that died instead...

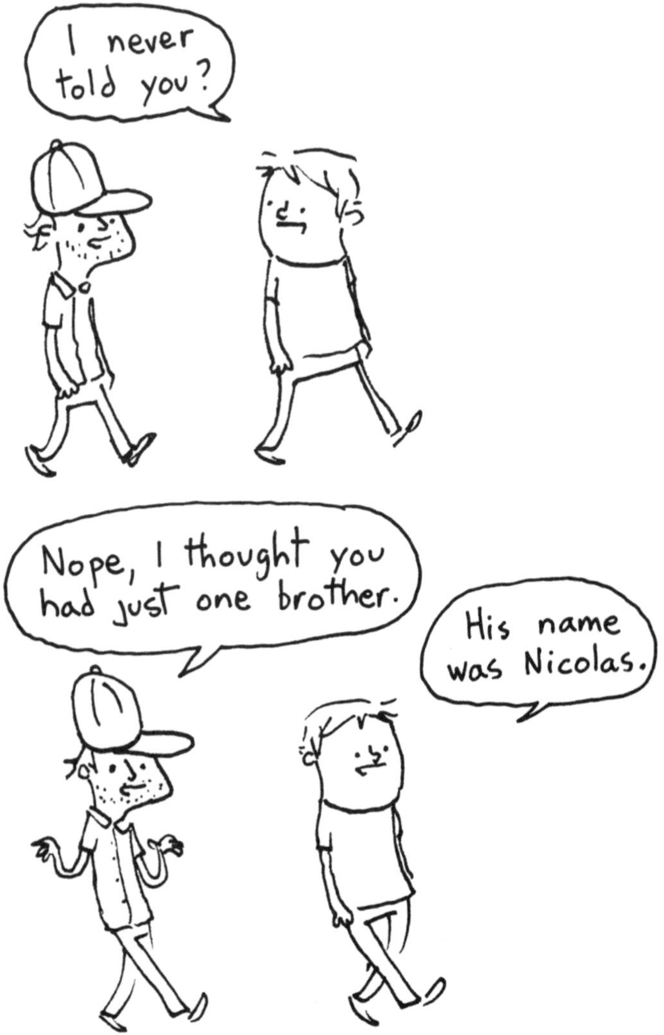
I never told you?
Nope, I thought you had just one brother.
His name was Nicolas.

Ha! That's cool!

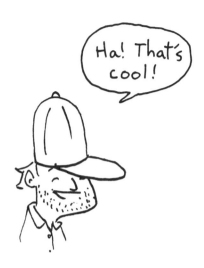

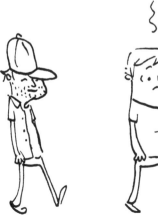

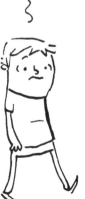

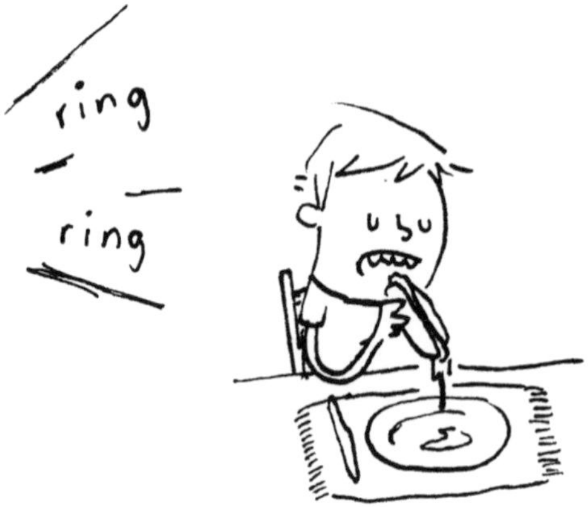
ring
ring

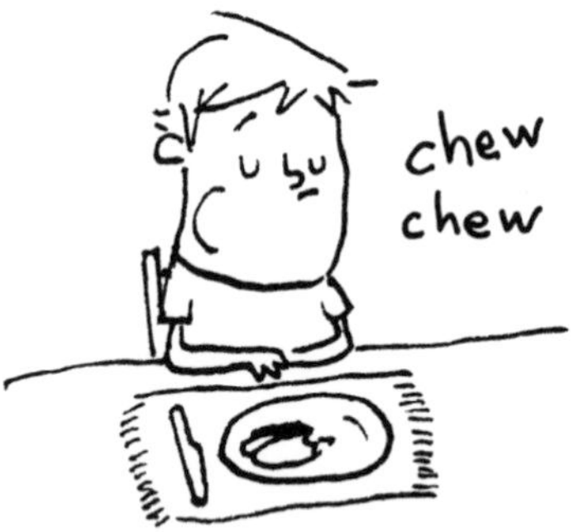
chew
chew

That was Pierre Lavoie on the phone... his son Raphaël is dead...

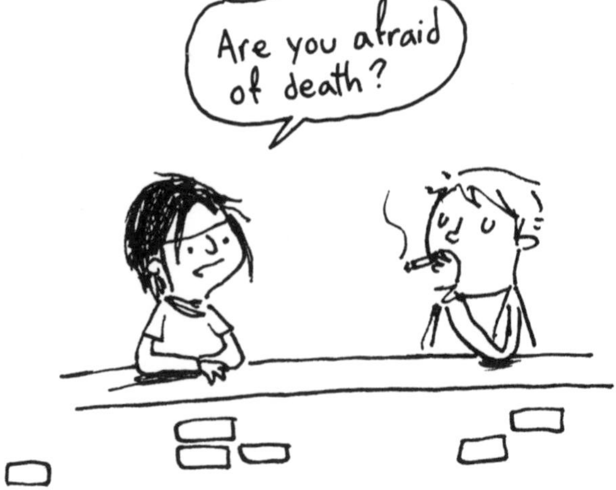
Are you afraid of death?

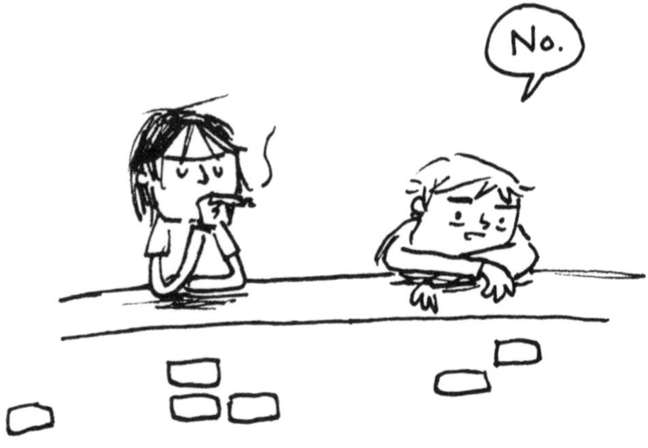
No.

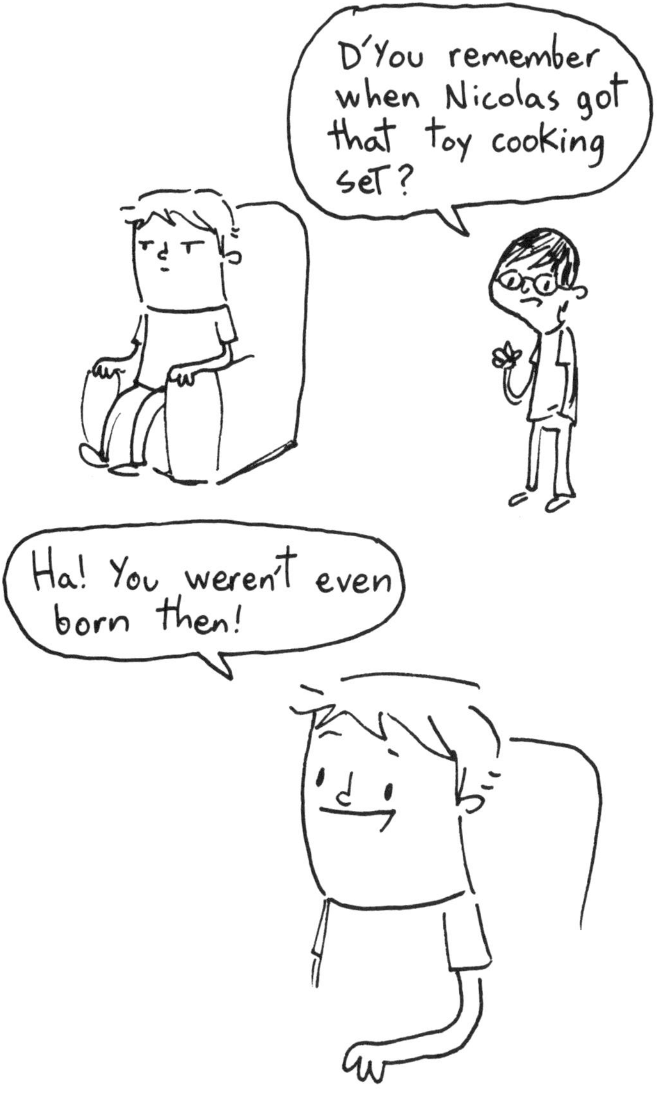
D'You remember when Nicolas got that toy cooking set?
Ha! You weren't even born then!

Yes I was! He said: "I'm gonna go cook something!"

You saw that in a video!!

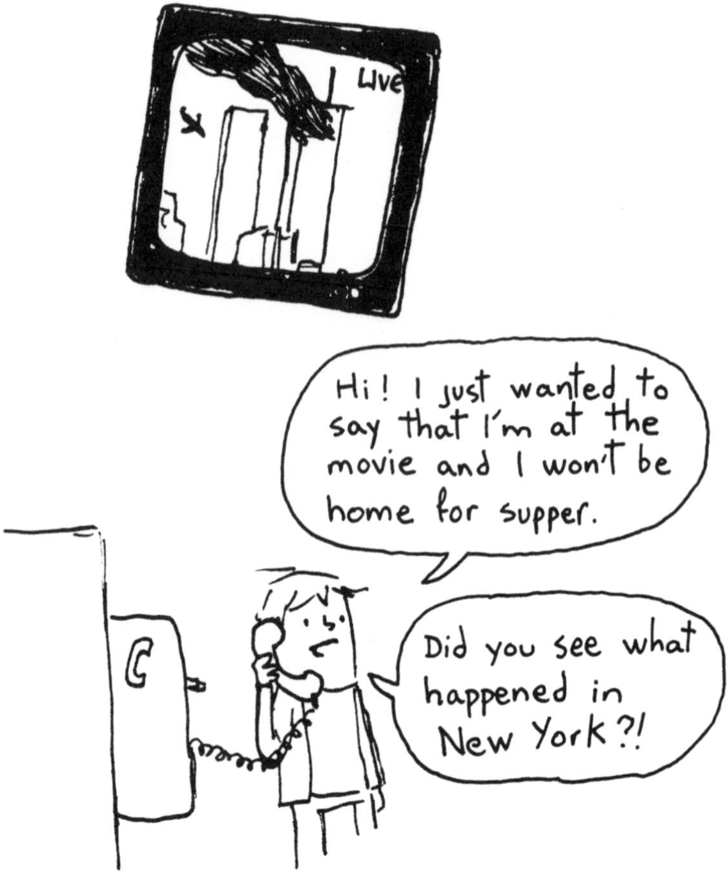
LIVE
Hi! I just wanted to say that I'm at the movie and I won't be home for supper.
Did you see what happened in New York?!

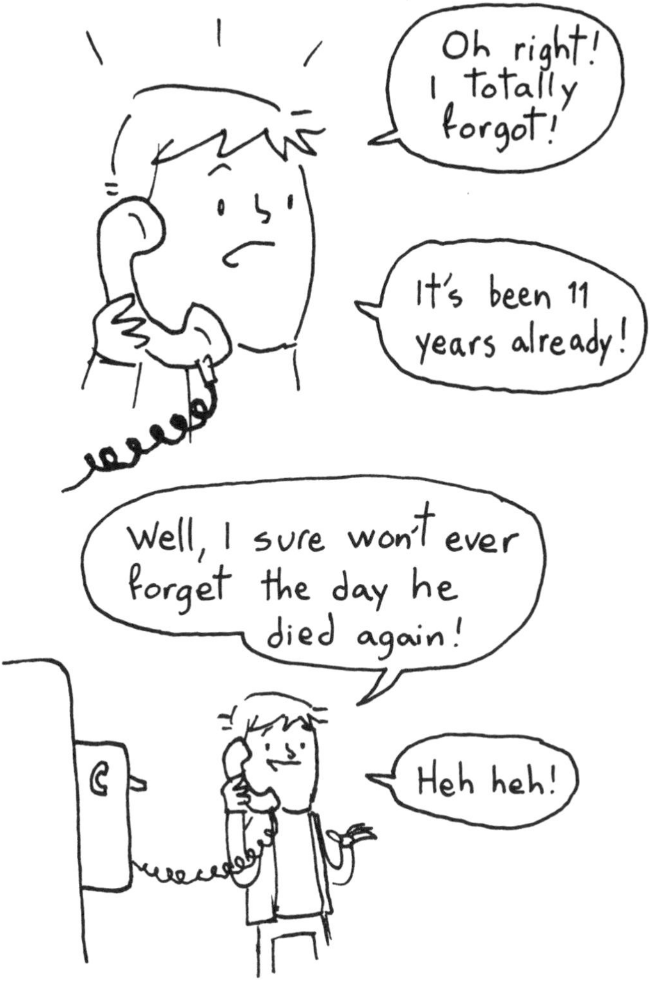
Oh right! I totally forgot!
It's been 11 years already!
Well, I sure won't ever forget the day he died again!
Heh heh!

I can't even remember what his voice sounded like.

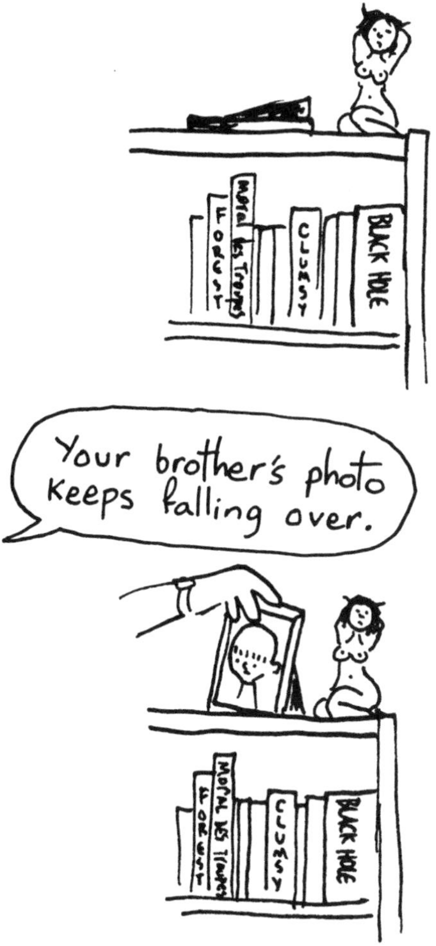
FOREST
CLUMSY
BLACK HOLE
Your brother's photo keeps falling over.
FOREST
CLUMSY
BLACK HOLE

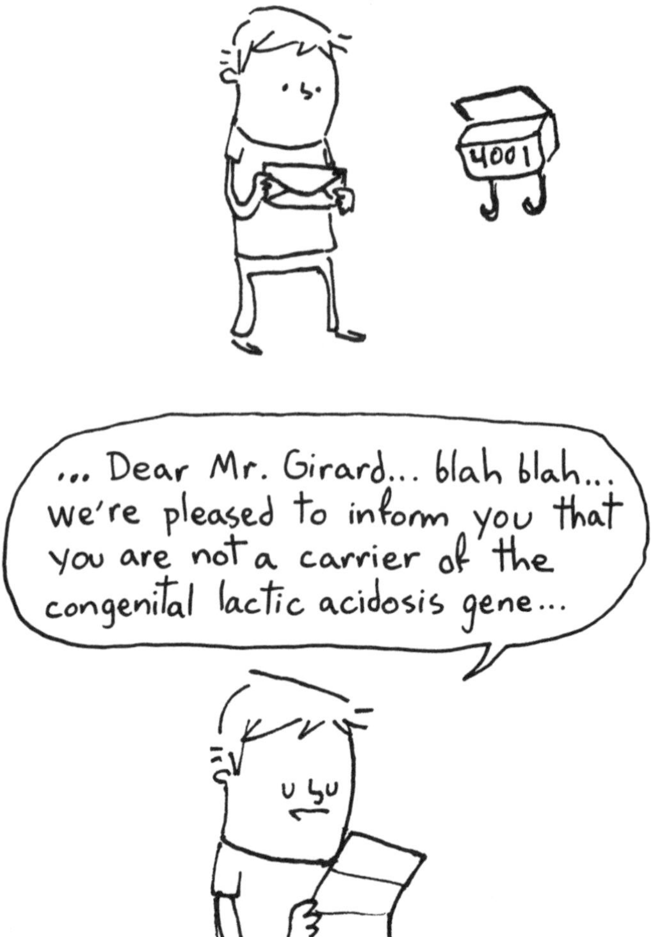
4001
... Dear Mr. Girard... blah blah... we're pleased to inform you that you are not a carrier of the congenital lactic acidosis gene...

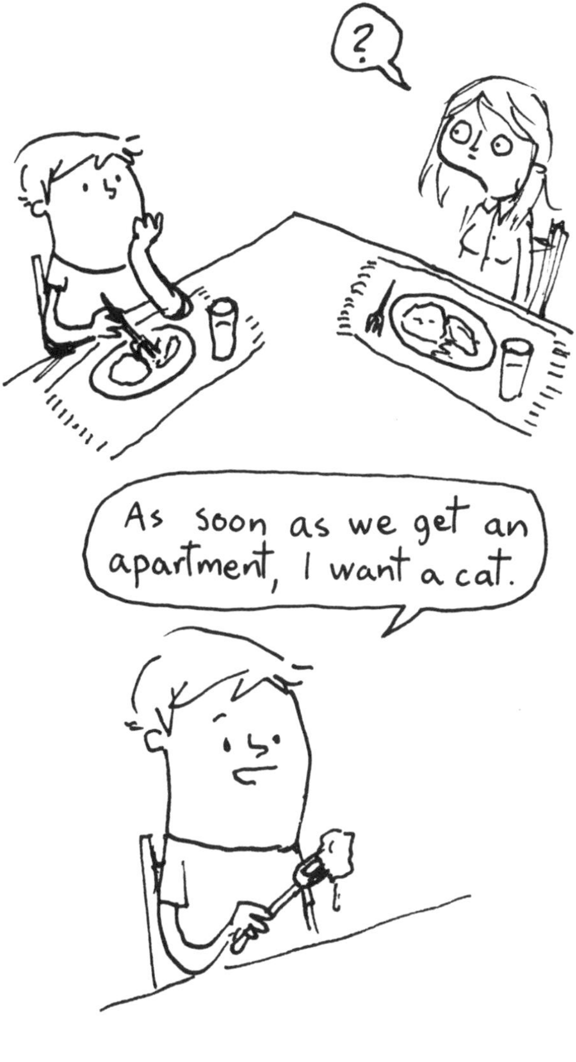
?
As soon as we get an apartment, I want a cat.

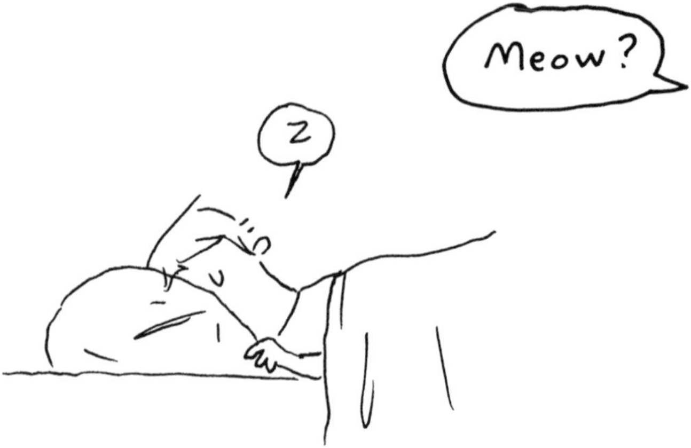
Meow?
z

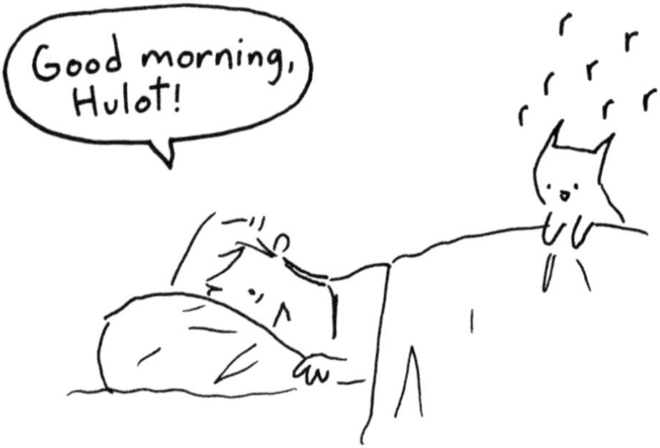
Good morning, Hulot!
r r r r r r r r

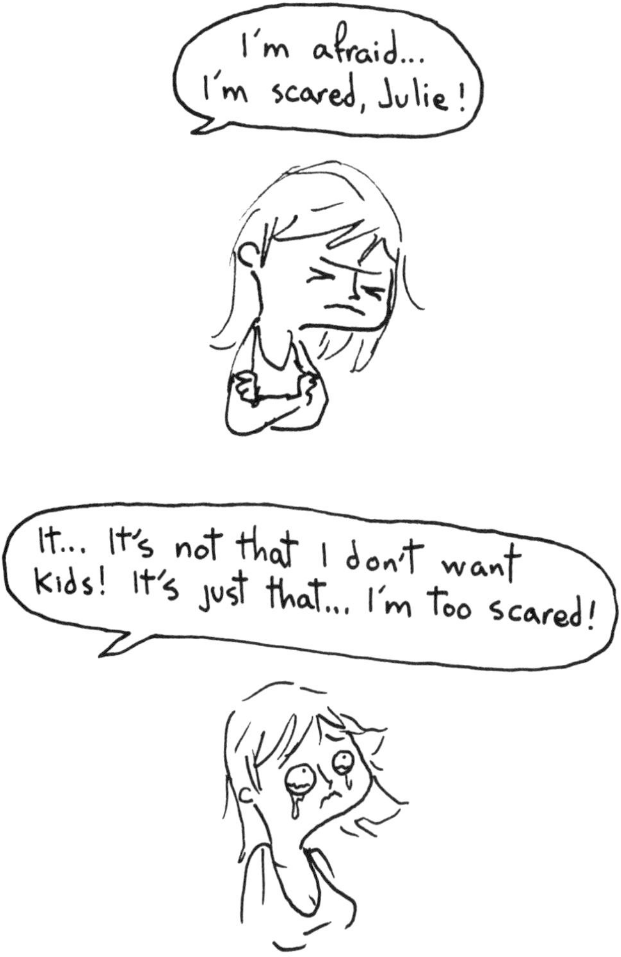
I'm afraid... I'm scared, Julie!
It... It's not that I don't want kids! It's just that... I'm too scared!

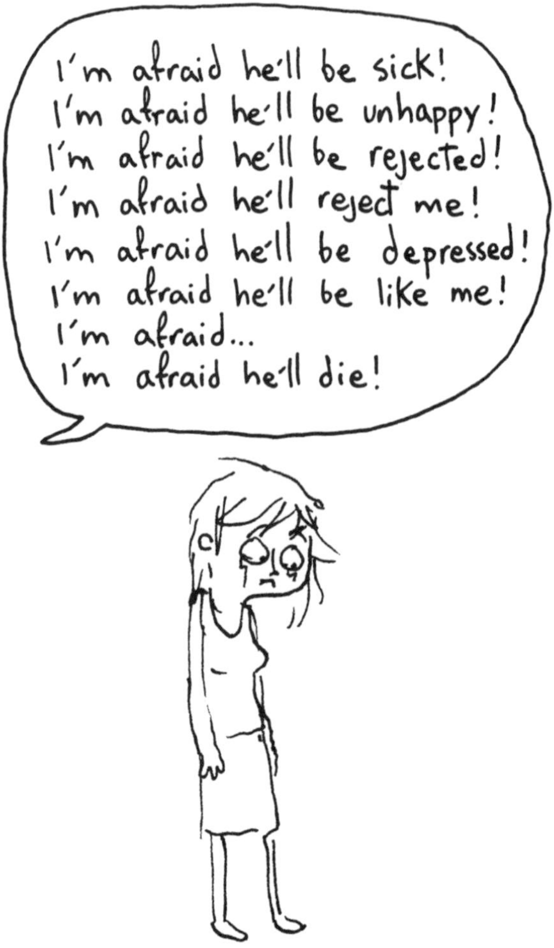
I'm afraid he'll be sick!
I'm afraid he'll be unhappy!
I'm afraid he'll be rejected!
I'm afraid he'll reject me!
I'm afraid he'll be depressed!
I'm afraid he'll be like me!
I'm afraid...
I'm afraid he'll die!

Sniff
...how about we start with one...

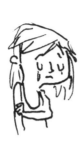

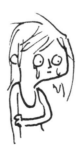

Julie! Jimmy wants to publish the comic I drew about my brother in his next anthology!

Wow! That's great!

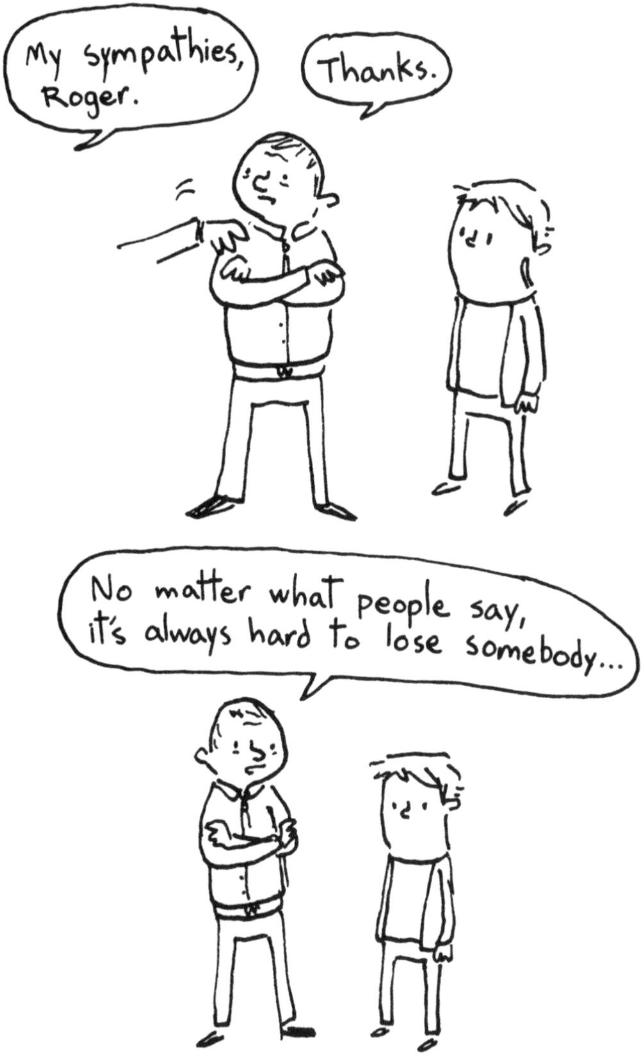
My sympathies, Roger.
Thanks.
No matter what people say, it's always hard to lose somebody...

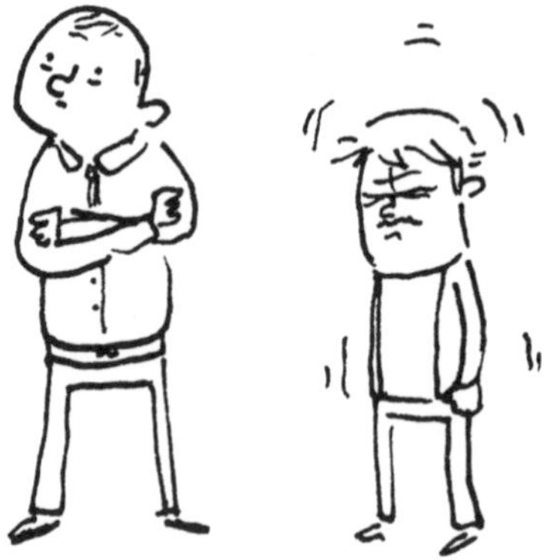

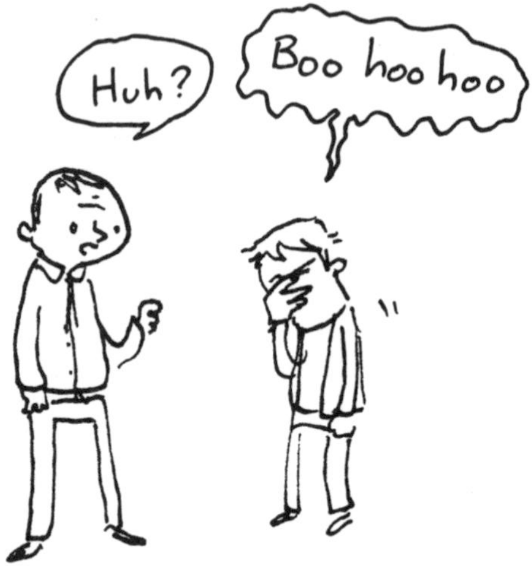
Huh?
Boo hoo hoo

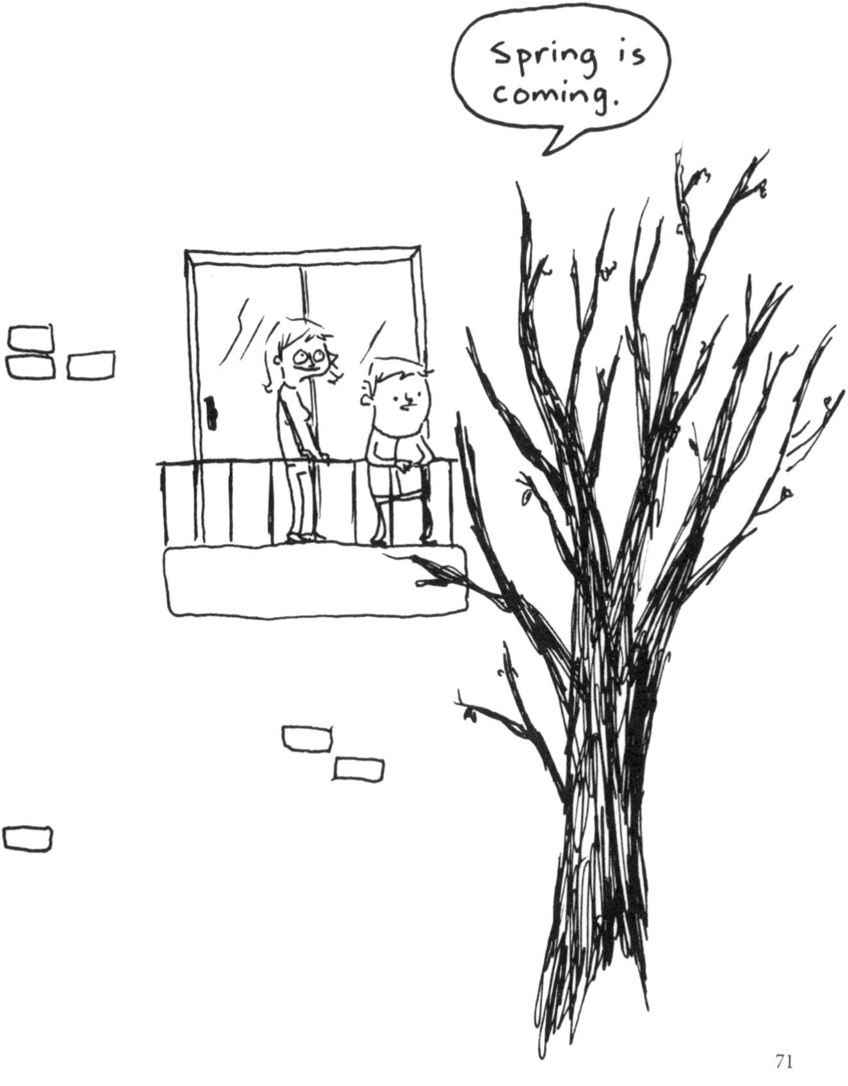
Spring is coming.

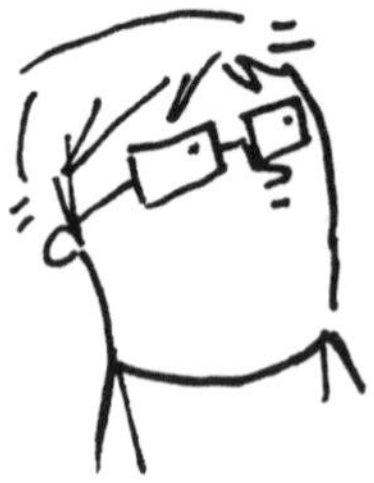

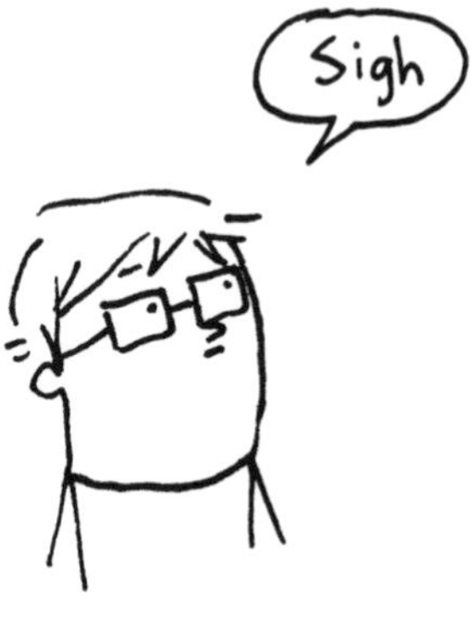
Sigh

If you knew how much I miss you today!

BEFORE

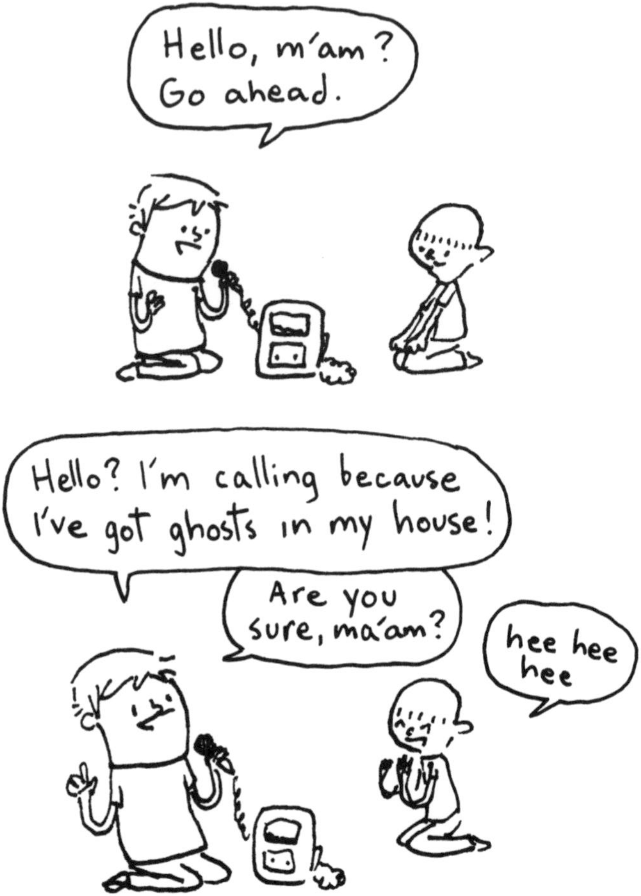
Hello, m'am? Go ahead.
Hello? I'm calling because I've got ghosts in my house!
Are you sure, ma'am?
hee hee hee

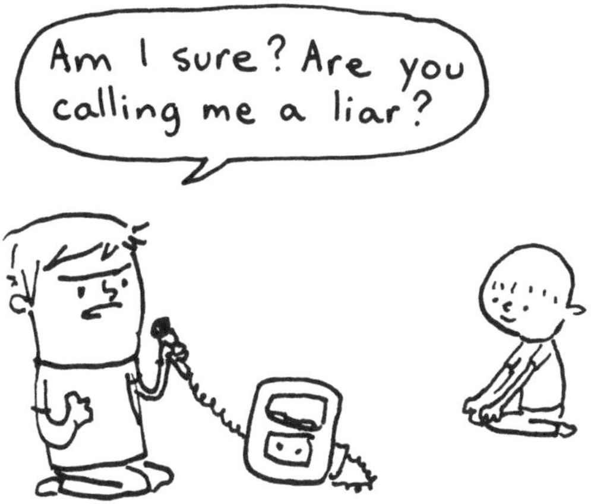
Am I sure? Are you calling me a liar?

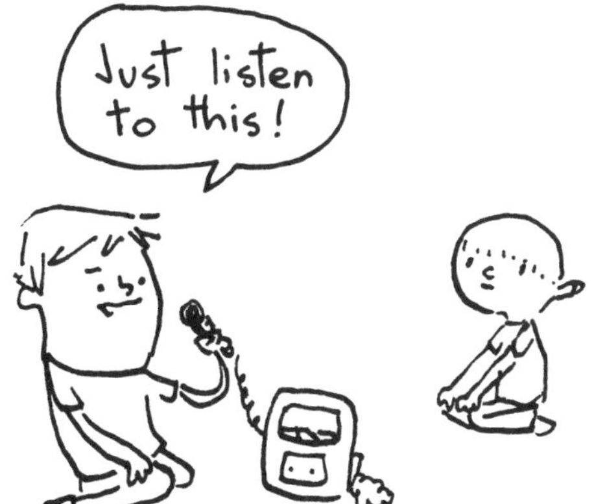
Just listen to this!

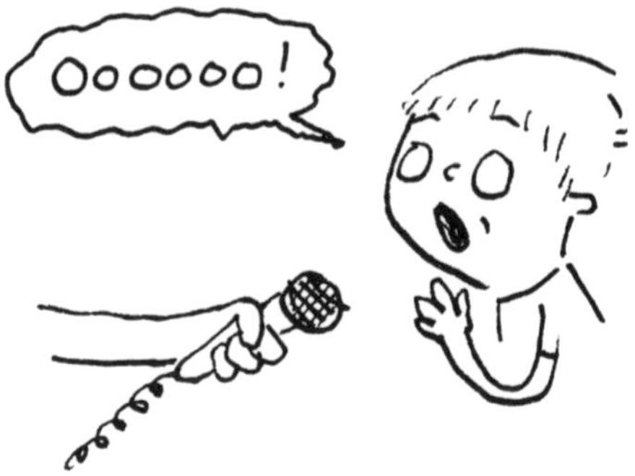
Oooooo!

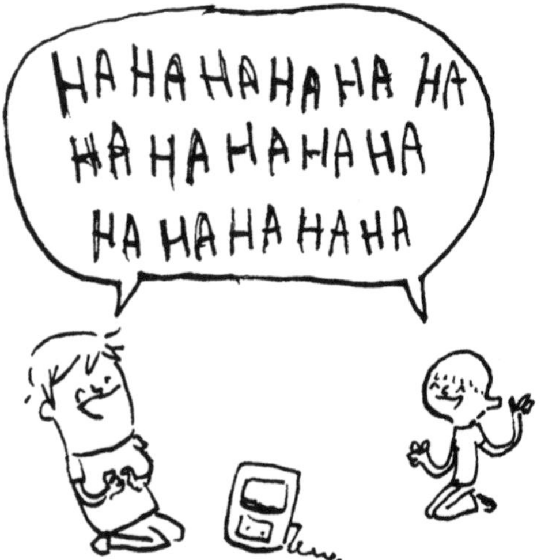
HA HA HA HA HA HA HA
HA HA HA HA HA HA
HA HA HA HA HA

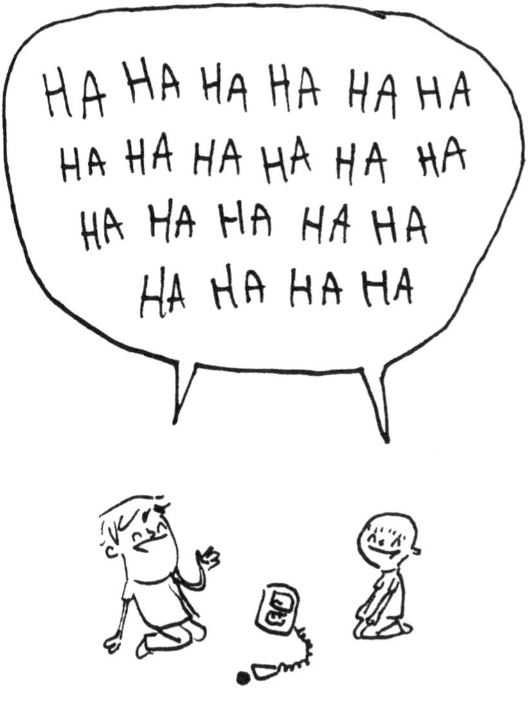
HA HA HA HA HA HA
HA HA HA HA HA HA
HA HA HA HA HA
HA HA HA HA

Afterword

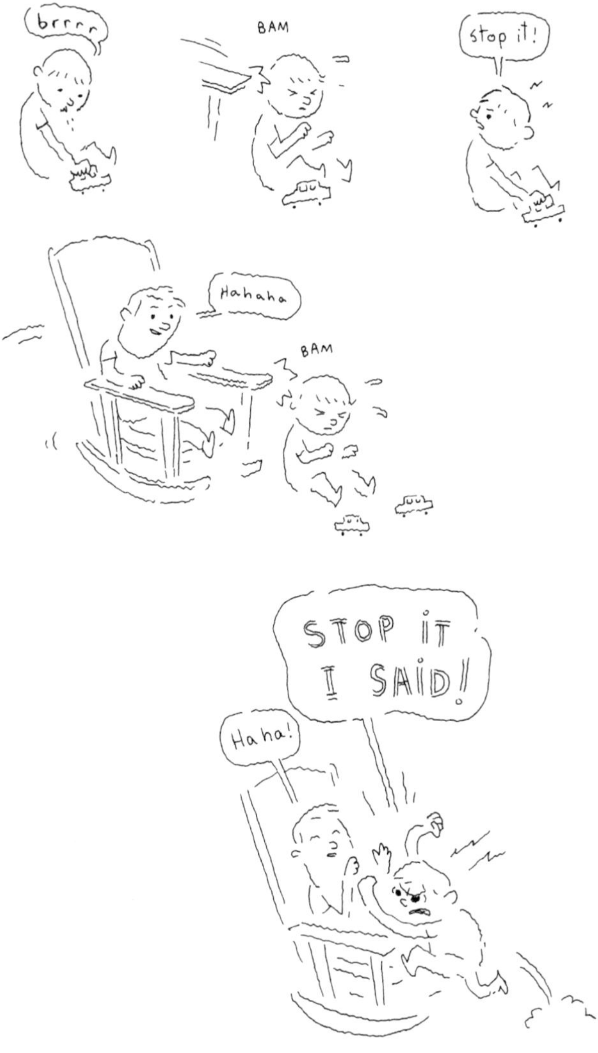
brrrr
BAM
stop it!
Hahaha
BAM
Haha!
STOP IT I SAID!

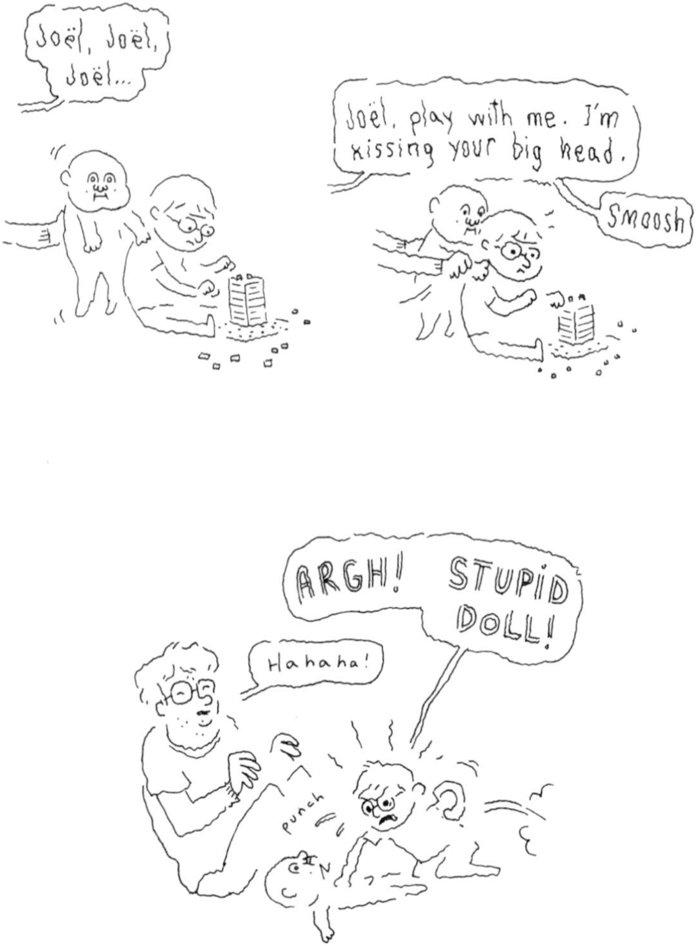
Joël, Joël, Joël...
Joël, play with me. I'm kissing your big head.
Smoosh
ARGH! STUPID DOLL!
Hahaha!
punch

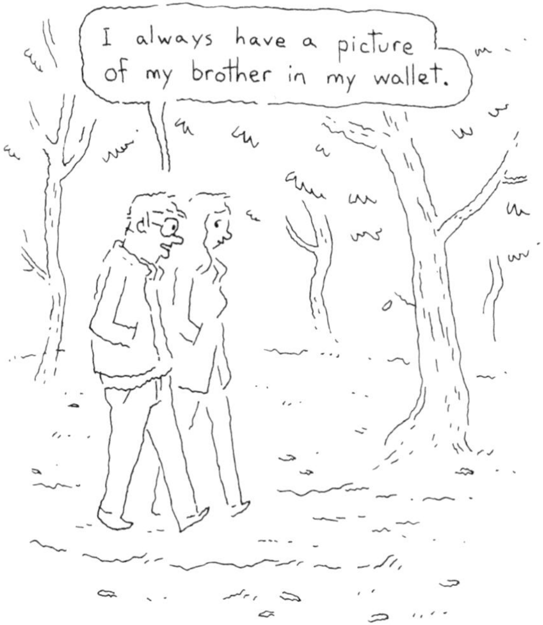
I always have a picture of my brother in my wallet.

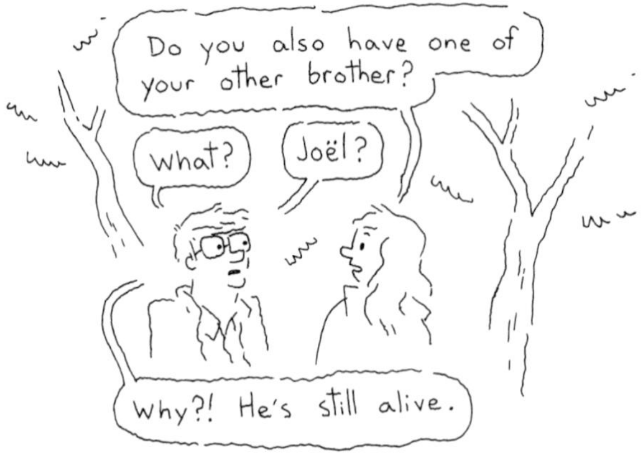
Do you also have one of your other brother?
What?
Joël?
Why?! He's still alive.

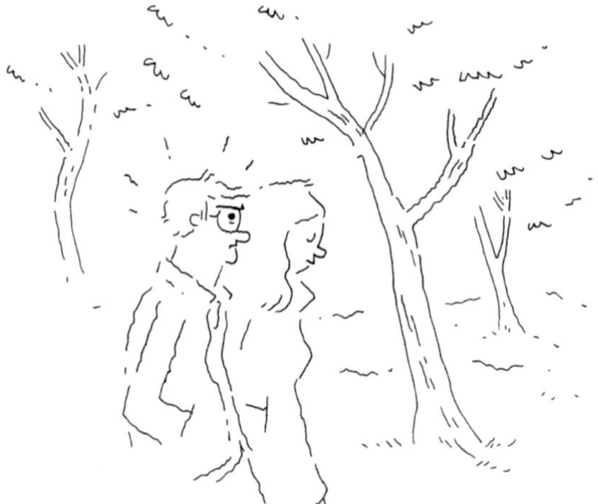

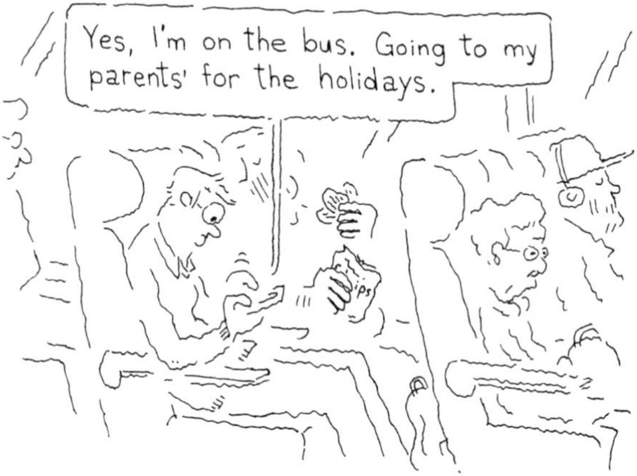
Yes, I'm on the bus. Going to my parents' for the holidays.

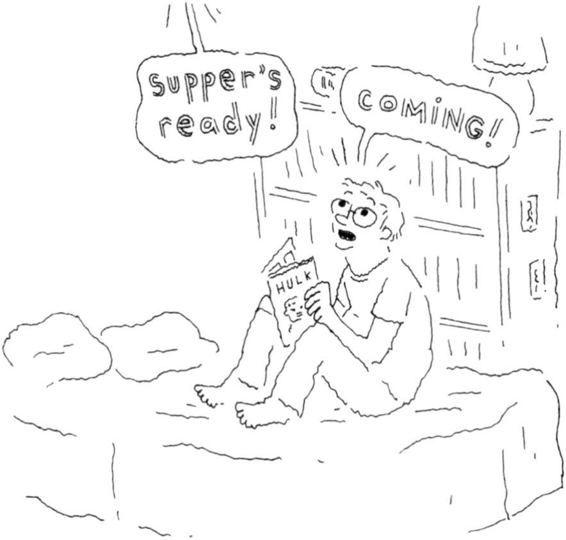
supper's ready!
COMING!
HULK

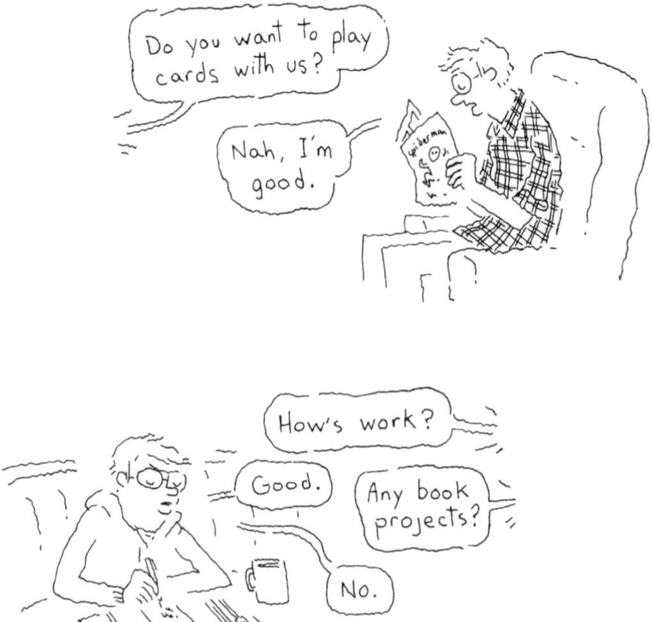
Do you want to play cards with us?
Nah, I'm good.
spiderman
How's work?
Good.
Any book projects?
No.

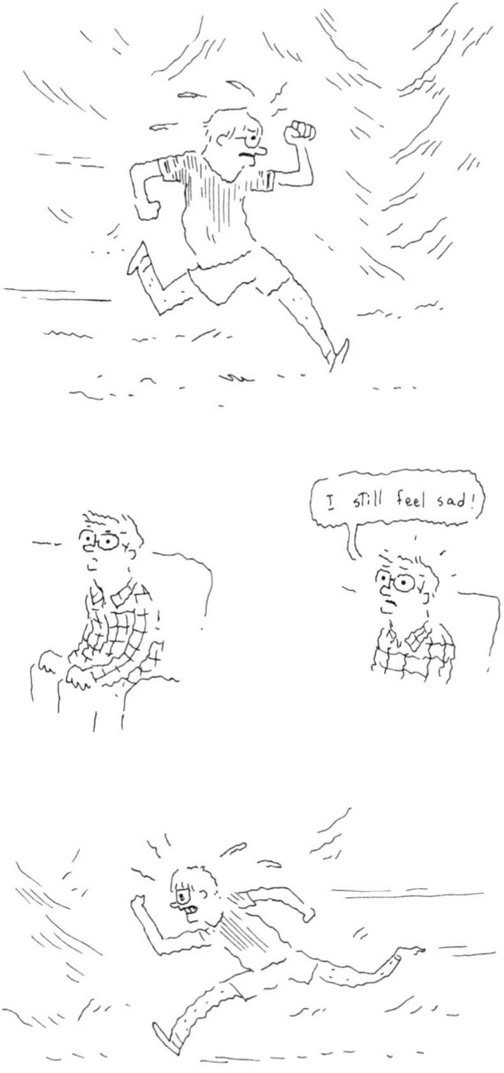
I still feel sad!

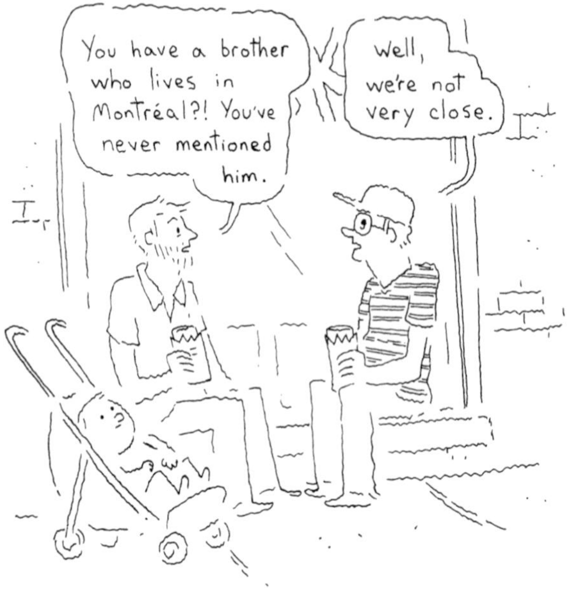
You have a brother who lives in Montréal?! You've never mentioned him.
Well, we're not very close.

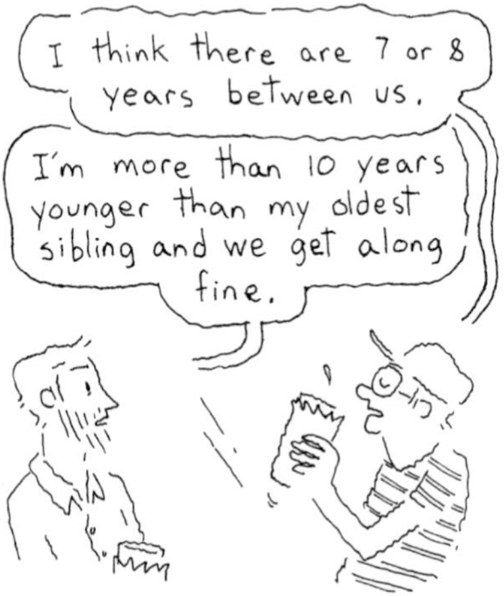
I think there are 7 or 8 years between us.
I'm more than 10 years younger than my oldest sibling and we get along fine.

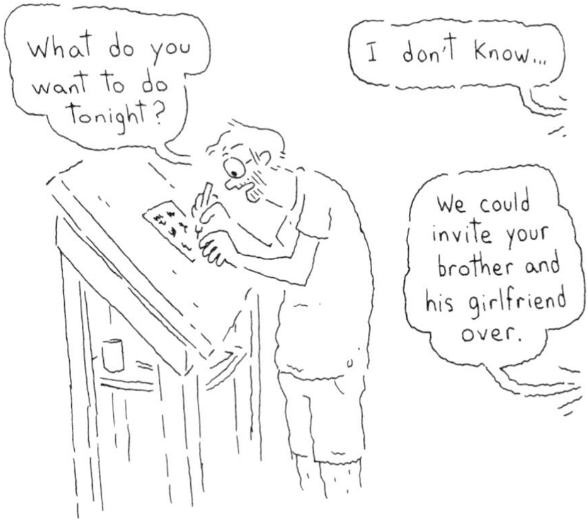
What do you want to do tonight?
I don't know...
We could invite your brother and his girlfriend over.

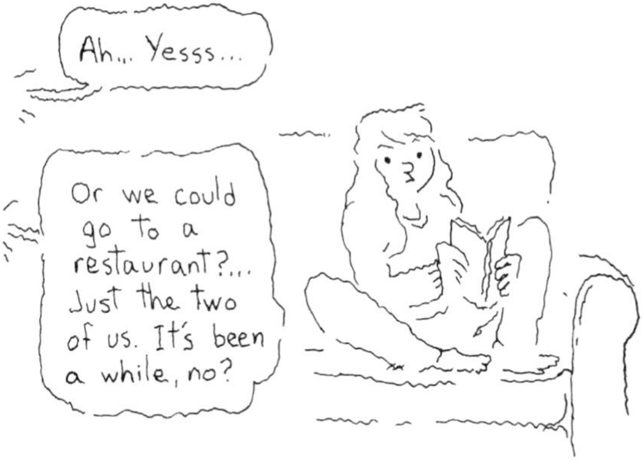
Ah... Yesss...
Or we could go to a restaurant?... Just the two of us. It's been a while, no?

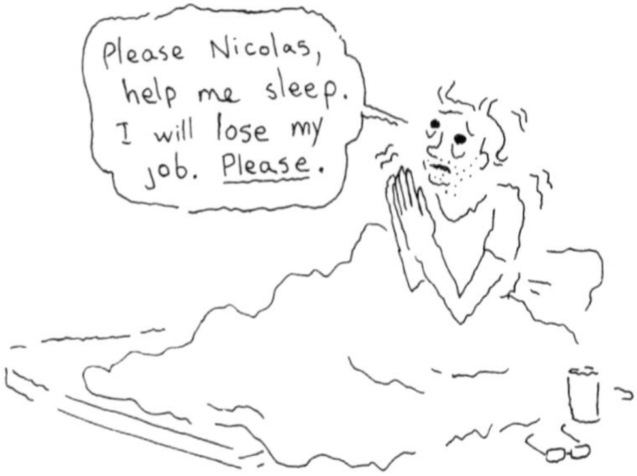
Please Nicolas, help me sleep. I will lose my job. Please.

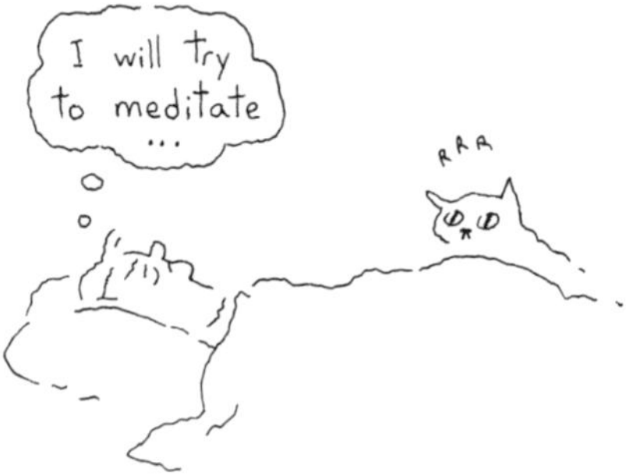
I will try to meditate ...
RRR

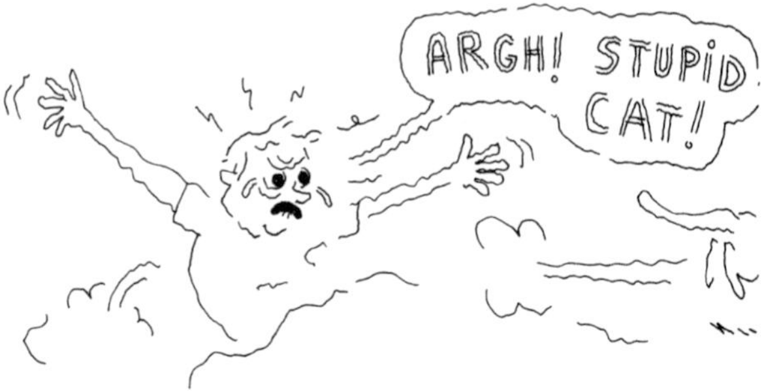
ARGH! STUPID CAT!

in therapy

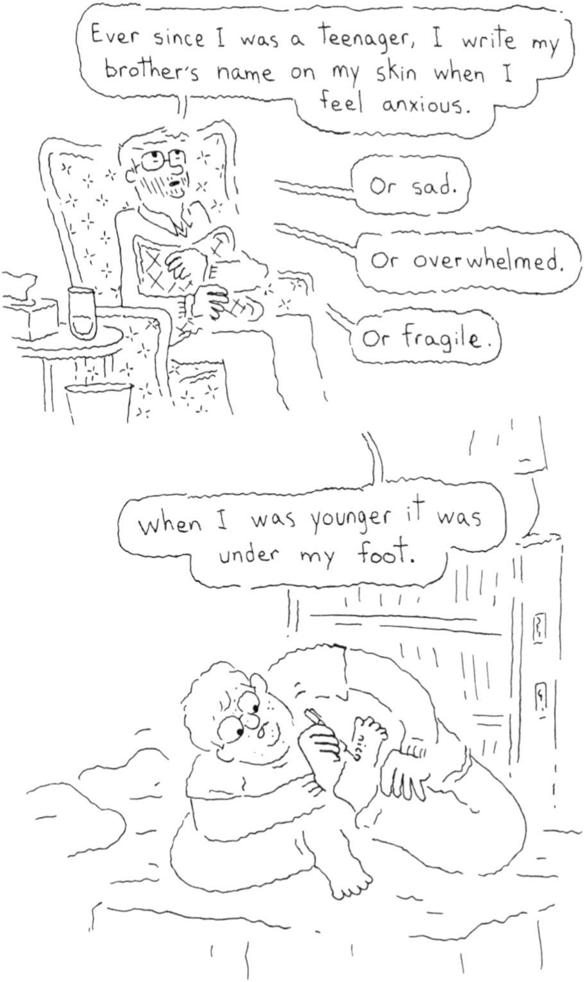
Ever since I was a teenager, I write my brother's name on my skin when I feel anxious.
Or sad.
Or overwhelmed.
Or fragile.
When I was younger it was under my foot.

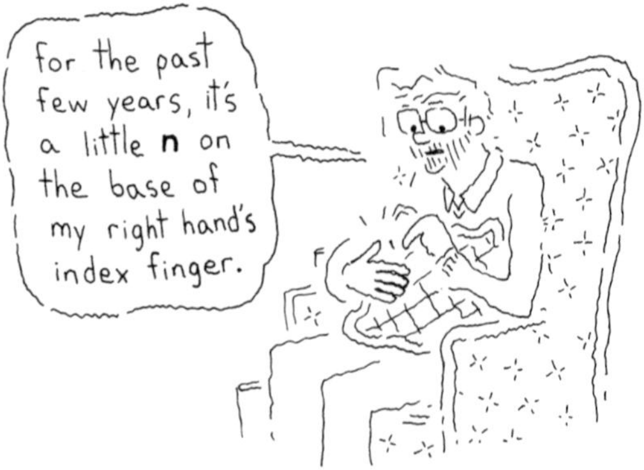
for the past few years, it's a little **n** on the base of my right hand's index finger.

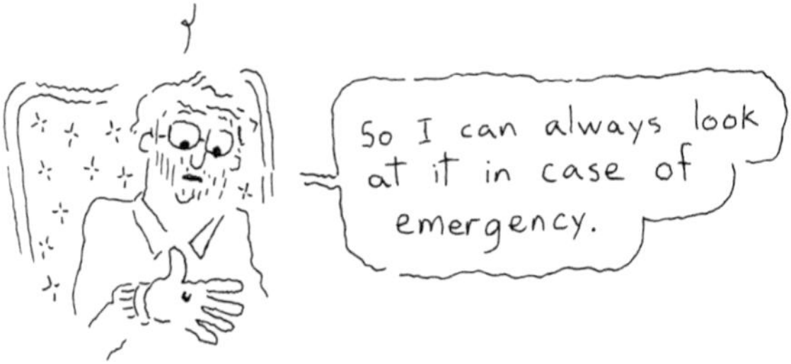
So I can always look at it in case of emergency.

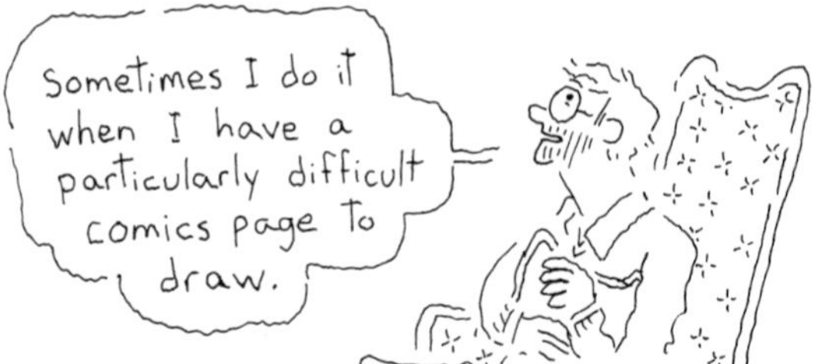
Sometimes I do it when I have a particularly difficult comics page to draw.

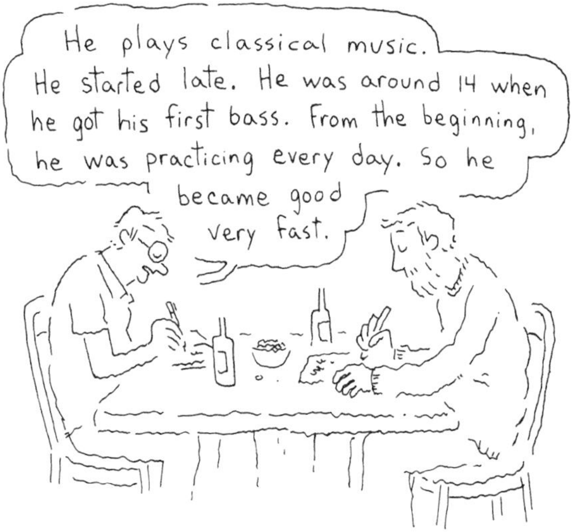
He plays classical music. He started late. He was around 14 when he got his first bass. From the beginning, he was practicing every day. So he became good very fast.

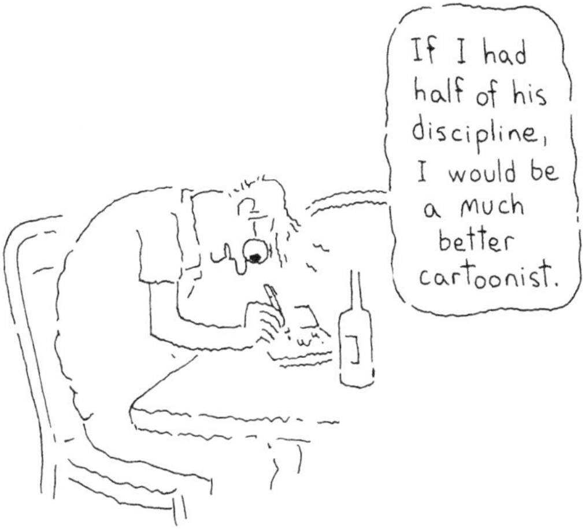
If I had half of his discipline, I would be a much better cartoonist.

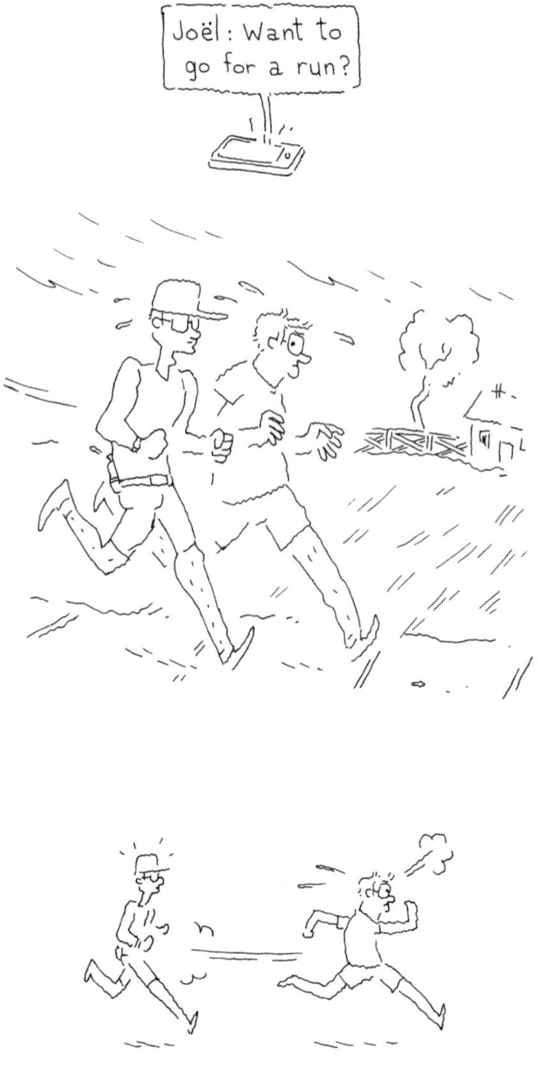
Joël: Want to go for a run?

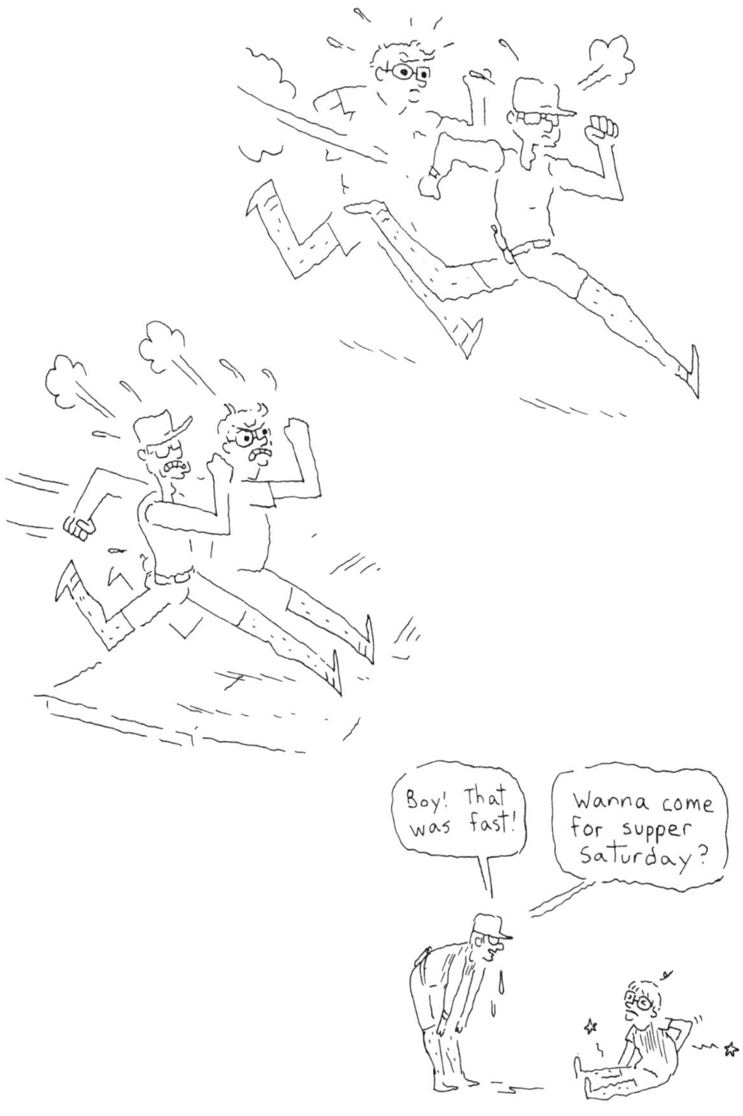
Boy! That was fast!
Wanna come for supper Saturday?

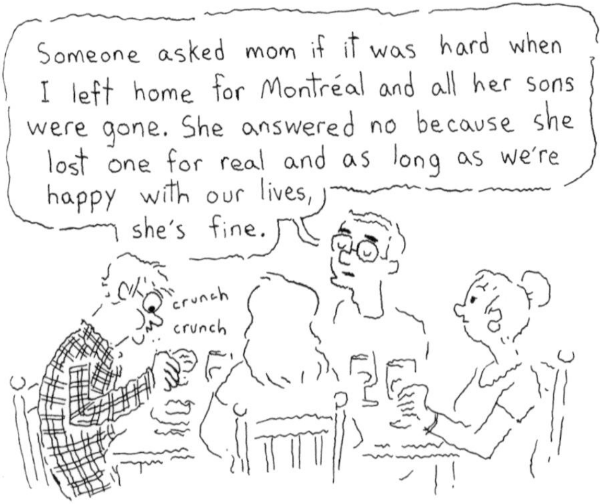
Someone asked mom if it was hard when I left home for Montréal and all her sons were gone. She answered no because she lost one for real and as long as we're happy with our lives, she's fine.
crunch
crunch

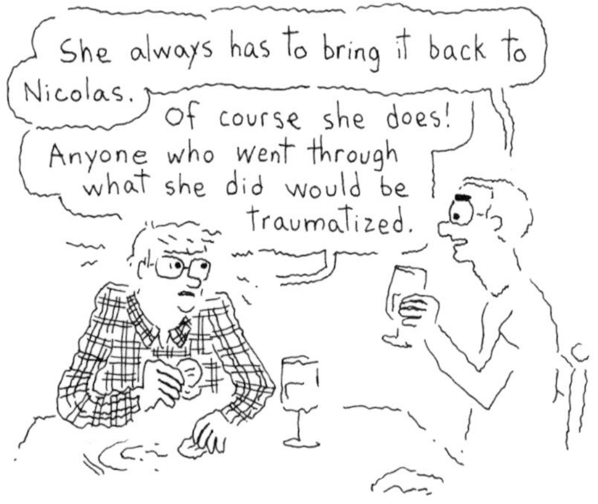
She always has to bring it back to Nicolas.
Of course she does! Anyone who went through what she did would be traumatized.

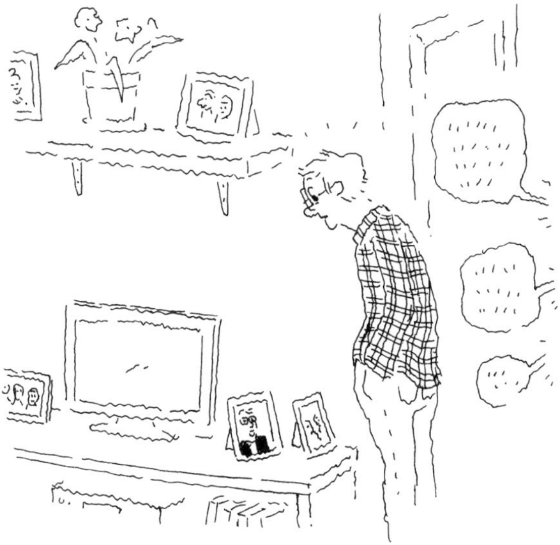

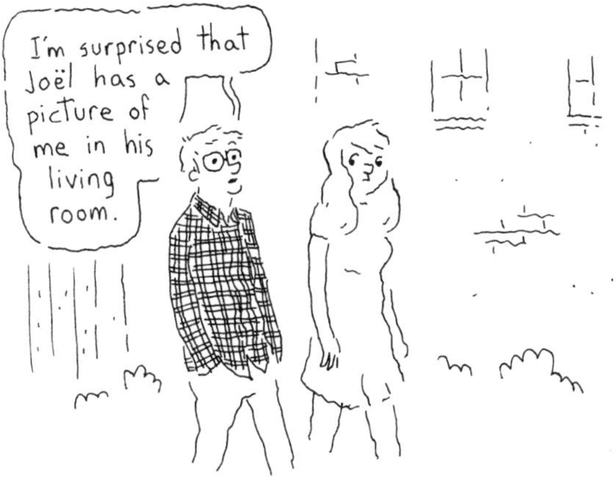
I'm surprised that Joël has a picture of me in his living room.

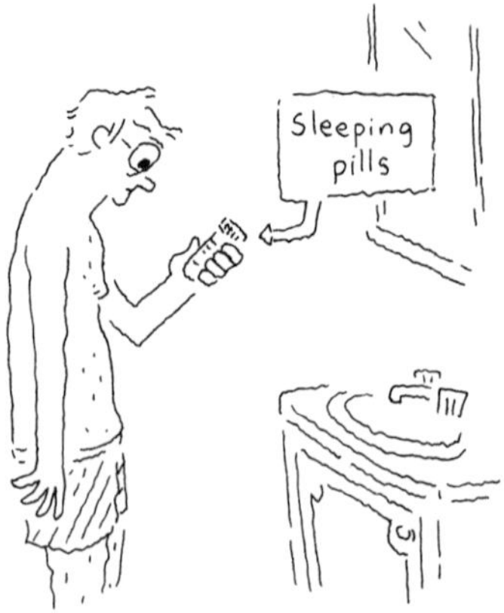
Sleeping pills

. . .

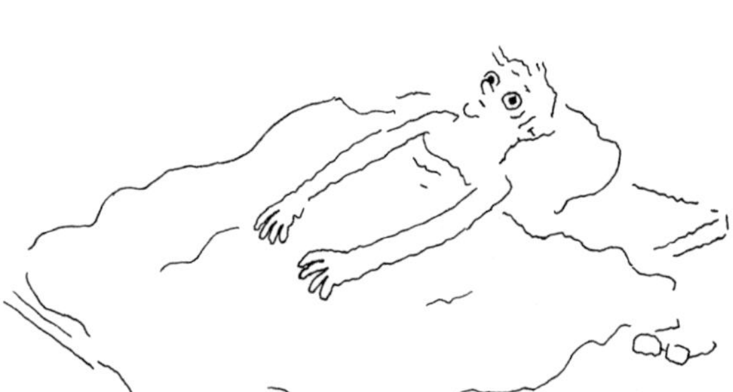

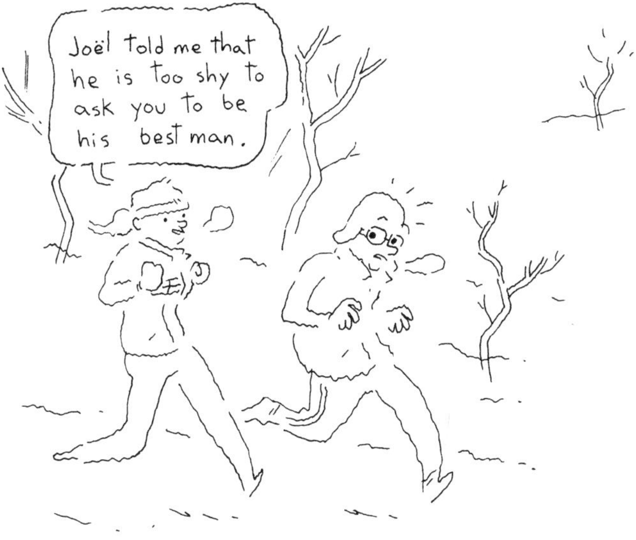
Joël told me that he is too shy to ask you to be his best man.

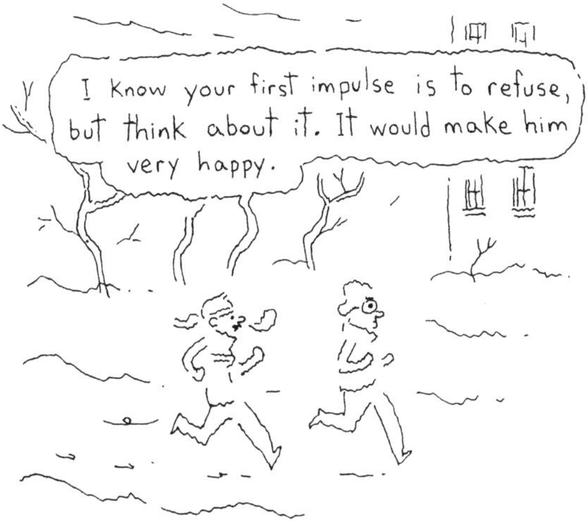
I know your first impulse is to refuse, but think about it. It would make him very happy.

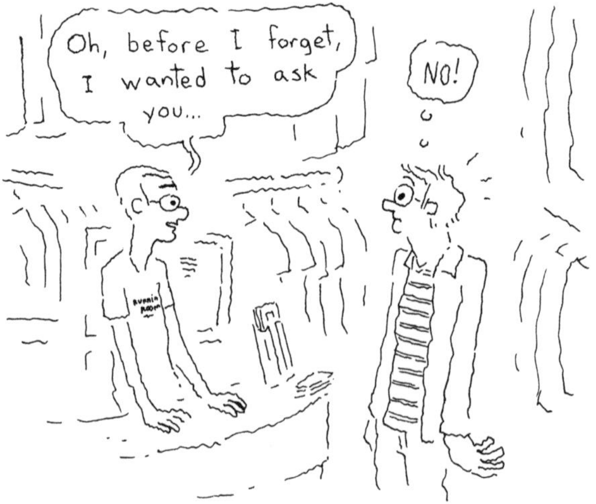
Oh, before I forget, I wanted to ask you...
NO!

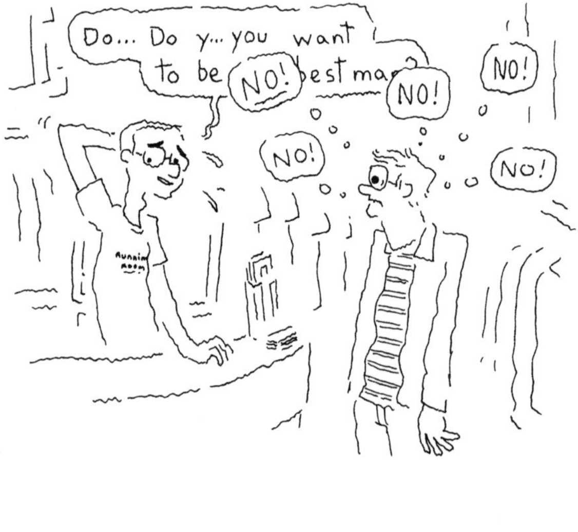
Do... Do y... you want to be
NO!
est ma
NO!
NO!
NO!
NO!

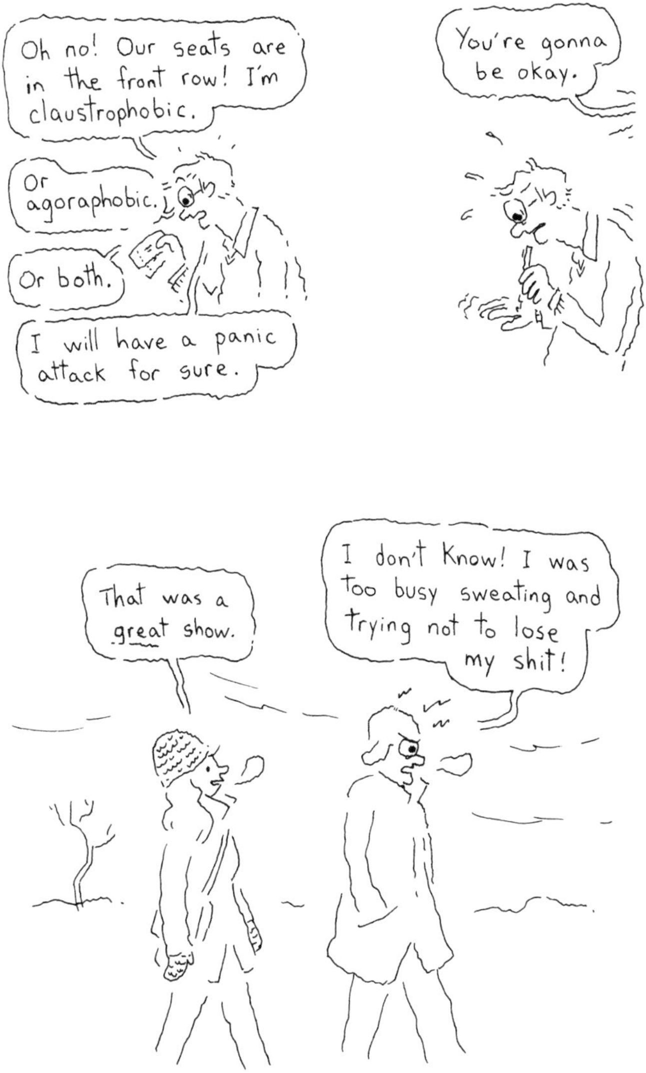
Oh no! Our seats are in the front row! I'm claustrophobic.
Or agoraphobic.
Or both.
I will have a panic attack for sure.
You're gonna be okay.
That was a great show.
I don't Know! I was too busy sweating and trying not to lose my shit!

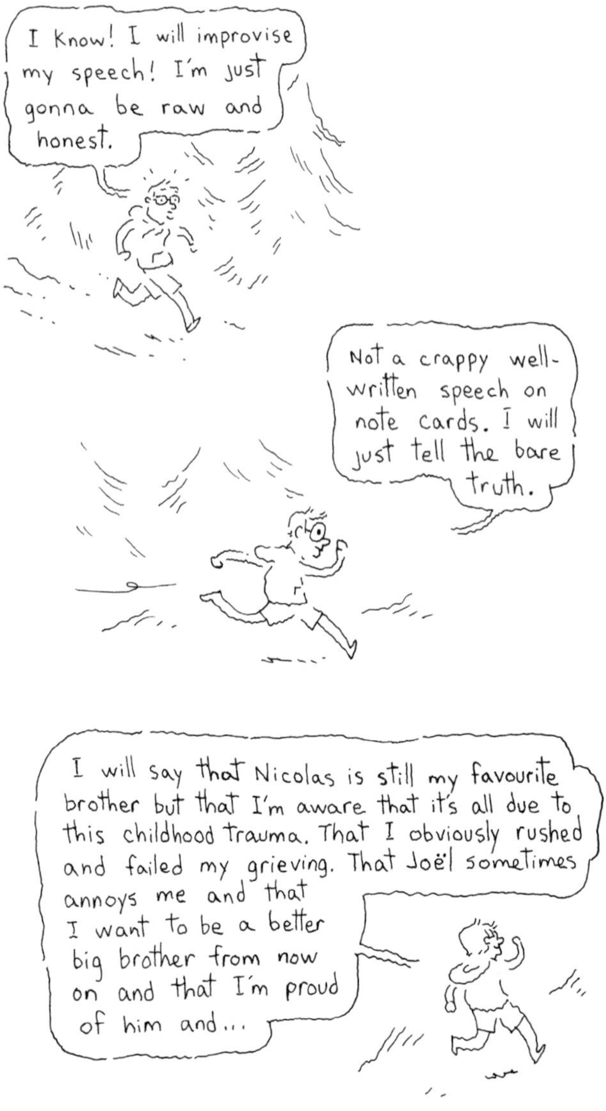
I know! I will improvise my speech! I'm just gonna be raw and honest.
Not a crappy well-written speech on note cards. I will just tell the bare truth.
I will say that Nicolas is still my favourite brother but that I'm aware that it's all due to this childhood trauma. That I obviously rushed and failed my grieving. That Joël sometimes annoys me and that I want to be a better big brother from now on and that I'm proud of him and...

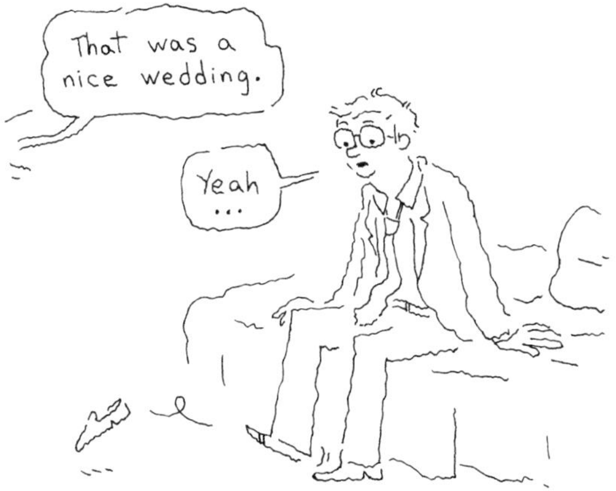
That was a nice wedding.
Yeah ...

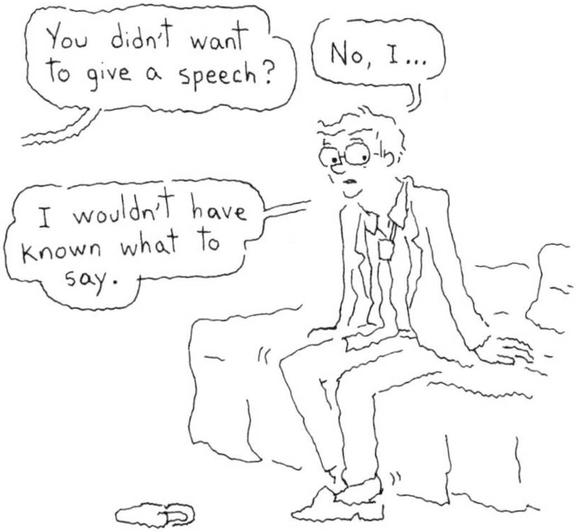
You didn't want to give a speech?
No, I...
I wouldn't have known what to say.

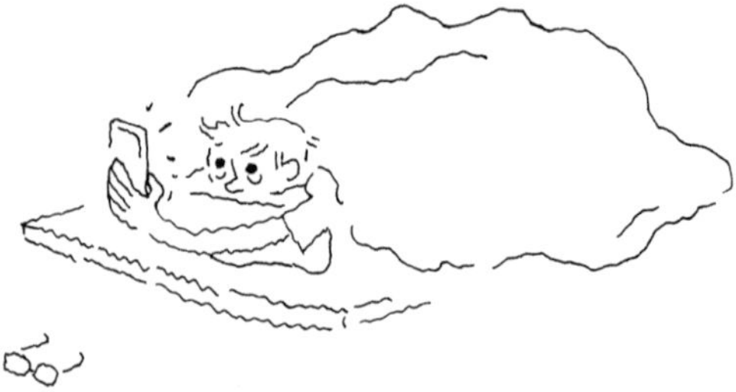

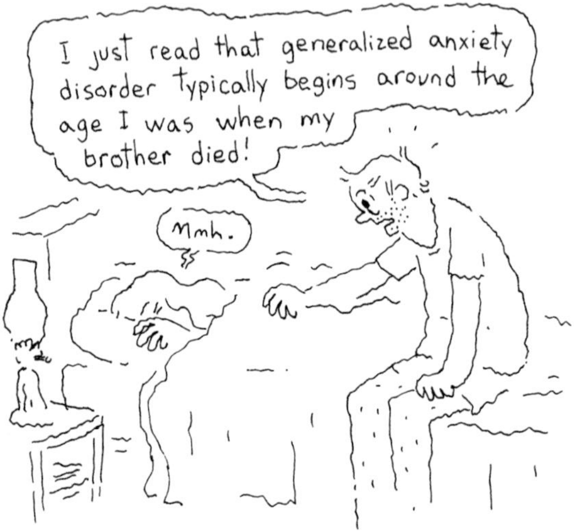
I just read that generalized anxiety disorder typically begins around the age I was when my brother died!
Mmh.

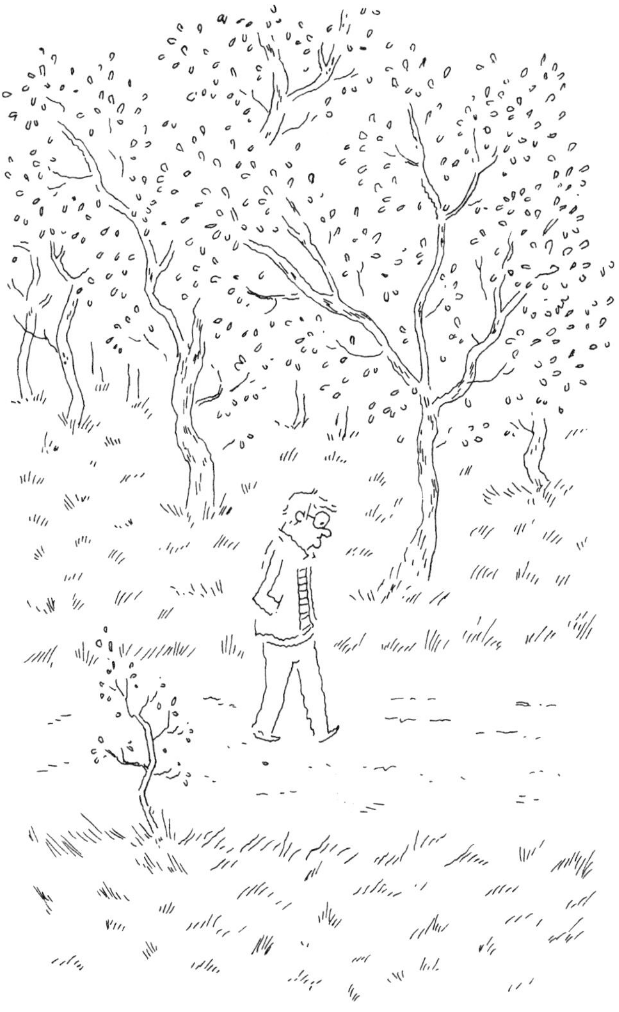

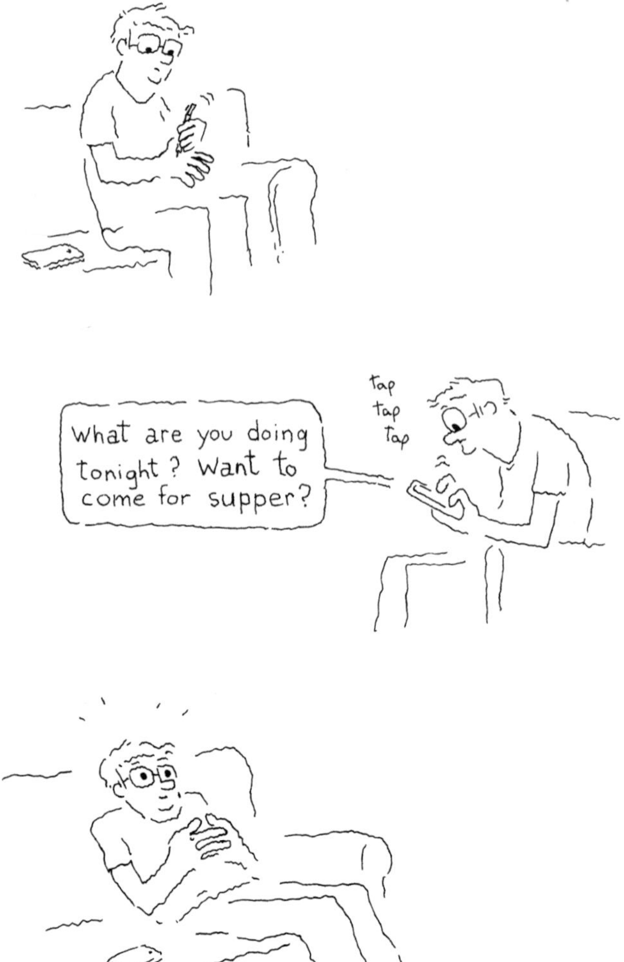
tap
tap
tap
What are you doing tonight? Want to come for supper?
pascal

drawnandquarterly.com

First edition: December 2008
Revised edition: September 2016
Printed in China
10 9 8 7 6 5 4 3 2 1

Library and Archives Canada Cataloguing in Publication: Girard, Pascal. [Nicolas. English] Nicolas/Pascal Girard; translator: Helge Dascher. Translation of: Nicolas. Previously published: 2008. ISBN 978-1-77046-262-5 (bound) 1. Girard, Pascal—Comic books, strips, etc. 2. Bereavement—Comic books, strips, etc. 3. Brothers—Comic books, strips, etc. 4. Graphic novels. I. Dascher, Helge, 1965–, translator II. Title. III. Title: Nicolas. English. PN6733.G57N5313 2016   741.5'971   C2016-900491-0

Published in the USA by Drawn & Quarterly, a client publisher of Farrar, Straus and Giroux. Orders: 888.330.8477. Published in Canada by Drawn & Quarterly, a client publisher of Raincoast Books. Orders: 800.663.5714. Published in the United Kingdom by Drawn & Quarterly, a client publisher of Publishers Group UK. Orders: info@pguk.co.uk.

Canada

Drawn & Quarterly acknowledges the support of the Government of Canada and the Canada Council for the Arts for our publishing program.

Drawn & Quarterly reconnaît l'aide financière du gouvernement du Québec par l'entremise de la Société de développement des entreprises culturelles (SODEC) pour nos activités d'édition. Gouvernement du Québec—Programme de crédit d'impôt pour l'édition de livres—Gestion SODEC.

Pascal Girard was born in Jonquière, QC, in 1981. He is the cartoonist of *Nicolas*, *Bigfoot*, *Reunion*, and *Petty Theft*. He has been nominated for the Ignatz Award and in 2011 won Best Book at the Doug Wright Awards for *Bigfoot*. He has been published in French by Les Éditions de la Pastèque, Éditions Delcourt, and Éditions Mécanique Générale. He lives in Montréal.